Star over Adobe

DOROTHY L. PILLSBURY

STAR
OVER
ADOBE

Illustrated by Richard Kurman

THE LIGHTNING TREE—*Jene Lyon, Publisher*
SANTA FÉ, NEW MEXICO   U.S.A.

BY DOROTHY L. PILLSBURY

No High Adobe
Adobe Doorways
Roots In Adobe
Star Over Adobe

STAR OVER ADOBE, Copyright © by The University of New Mexico Press, 1963. All rights reserved. Reprinted by special arrangement with The University of New Mexico Press.

Library of Congress Catalog Card No. 63-21376

ISBN: 0-89016-068-6 (PA)   ISBN: 0-89016-074-0 (CL)

MANUFACTURED IN THE UNITED STATES OF AMERICA

First Lightning Tree Edition—1983

THE LIGHTNING TREE   *Jene Lyon, Publisher*
P.O. Box 1837   Santa Fé, New Mexico 87504-1837   U.S.A.

Contents

Star over Adobe

Three-Culture Christmas

In the midst of a changing world, we keep a three-culture Christmas in northern New Mexico. Three peoples of us live here in the shadow of great mountains. Our skins are bronze, or brown, or white depending on whether we live in a sun-mellowed Indian pueblo, in a remote Spanish village, or in an "Anglo" and Spanish town like Santa Fe.

Each of us keeps his own Christmas according to the traditions of our three different peoples. But through the years there has been much mingling of customs until Christmas in northern New Mexico has become a heady mixture of all our folkways.

On the afternoon before Christmas, we look out on the wintry landscape and become suddenly stricken with nostalgia. Most of us are in the midst of preparations for our own Christmas. We keep thinking about huddled adobe houses in many a Spanish village back in the hills where dwarf piñon forests sparkle with snow. We remember the aroma of an entire village where piñon smoke floats like incense from each squat chimney. We hear the tinkle of goats' bells in corrals and the strumming of a lone guitar floating down the snowy roads. Almost before we know it, we find ourselves in a car and headed for Truchas or Trampas or a dozen other likely places.

The village beside the little frozen stream looks like a mica-spattered Christmas card. Weather-beaten doors are shut against the cold, but in many a window blooms a forest of geranium plants in old tin cans. Between scarlet, pink, or white blooms may stand a hand-carved saint or angel gazing mild-ly at a straw-filled, doll-sized manger. Children run back and forth between the houses, slamming doors behind them. But not so quickly that we miss delectable odors—meat balls simmering in a sauce *muy, muy picante* and little three-cornered pies bursting their seams with apples and brown sugar!

Night has fallen darkly over old Santa Fe as the homeward-bound car tops the last ridge of hills. Through a mesh of lightly falling snowflakes, all the buildings of the ancient capital seem etched against the sky in strokes of light. Flat roofs and archways leading to snowy gardens, squat chimneys, and out-of-plumb walls are outlined in shadowy candle gleam from sand-ballasted paper-bag lanterns that give the effect of parchment shades.

In the ancient plaza, three peoples cluster around the Anglo Christmas tree. Rosy-cheeked, bemittened children tug at restraining parental arms. Spanish-speaking *muchachos*, shepherded by black-shawled grandmothers, stand big-eyed, the snow clinging to their long, dark eyelashes. Indians in from nearby pueblos stalk about taking in the sights. The women's high white boots look whiter than the snow. Their shawls of red, purple, and green, and the men's bright headbands, make splashes of color under the lights. Christmas in three tongues, the folkways of our three peoples, unite to make beautiful the Night of Peace in old Santa Fe.

Santa Fe Aniversario

Here, as Christmas follows Christmas, I like to remember how, almost a quarter of a century ago, I walked down the snowy Acequia Madre with my first Santa Fe cat, Koshare, in my arms and into the Little Adobe House that was to become the scene of a new way of living.

The trail to that little house spreads backward a long way, now that I have the perspective of more than two decades. It spreads to years of work in a West Coast city, to junketing from Alaska to Mexico, and from the Grand Teton country to the blue bay of Monterey. Always, I realize now, I was looking each region over with an eye to a location for a little house, where I could live simply in beautiful natural surroundings with the mechanics of mundane living reduced to their absolute minimum.

Then, suddenly, out of a blue sky, I was able to do more than cast a speculative eye on little houses to shelter a simple way of living. As I look back now, every event is as significant and plain as a well-charted map. I found myself in Albuquerque, using the place as a kind of springboard into realms I had never dreamed existed, although my junketings had brought me several times into the state.

Always in my years of social work in the West Coast city, I had kept a special interest in the Spanish-speaking people who came to my professional attention. In northern New Mexico, I picked up that Spanish thread again, but with what a difference! This thread at that time comprised sixty percent of the state's meager population. It was not a minority group. It was woven into the highly colored land.

I picked up this Spanish thread with unreasonable delight. I followed it into the state university. I pursued it down into Old Mexico and to the islands of the Caribbean. I returned, knowing that the thread here in a perfect setting was my goodly portion.

After three years, the dream of a little house, that had faded with all the pursuit, returned brighter and more compelling than ever. It became so insistent that one day I packed my bag and started for Santa Fe, a place I scarcely knew. There I would first rent a little house.

I went from the bus to a hotel, thinking it would take several days to find even a house to rent. As soon as I had deposited my bag in the room, I started to walk up a long road that led to cloud-shadowed mountains, but which held few houses. As I walked, I found myself almost shouting, "I am home! I am home!" At last I returned to the plaza and found a real estate office. In one minute I had explained what I wanted, the next I was in a car, and in a twinkling I was writing a check for the first month's rent for a little house in an adobe placita.

I lived in that little house all the year I was going over a wide area in search of a house to buy. I wanted such simple things as a glimpse of nearby mountains, a water ditch, fruit trees and a lilac bush or two, and, of course, a thick-walled little house.

Then, one day, a strange man in a beret stopped me on the street and asked if I would like to rent a little adobe house on the outskirts of town. He and his wife were both called to war work and his wife was already in Washington.

I told him I wanted to buy a house. The man in the beret looked at me aghast. "That house belongs to my wife," he shouted. "She and an old Indian built it with their own hands. It is her baby. She wouldn't sell—well, she just wouldn't sell."

In the afternoon, I walked up in the dirt-road district to look at the place. It seemed miles out in the country in spite of the short walk. Mountains spread, peak against peak, not far away to the east. There were two hundred feet of lilac bushes. I counted two peach trees, one pear, and one wild plum. A white locust and two silver maples were thrown in for good measure. There was not one, but three adobe houses.

No one was about. Brazenly I peered in the windows of the first house and decided it must be rented to a musical person, as a violin, a grand piano, and a big yellow cat seemed to take up most of the little adobe. The next house, which the man with the beret was leaving, looked rather discouraging viewed from the windows, as he was evidently packing the family belongings in boxes for storage. The third house was probably a one-room workshop. But I had counted, altogether, four corner fireplaces.

I went back to the rented house and tried to give up the thought of four corner fireplaces and two hundred feet of lilac bushes. I walked the floor. At ten that night, flashlight in hand, I negotiated the dark unlighted windings of the dirt-road district and rapped on the door of the second adobe. The man in the beret was writing a letter to his wife.

"I've never bought a house in all my life," I explained. "But I can't give this place up. Please wire your wife at my expense and ask her what is her lowest cash price for the place."

The man in the beret expostulated. "It's a waste of time and money," he snorted. "My wife wouldn't sell. It's her . . . "

"Yes," I agreed. "I know it's her baby and that she and an old Indian built it brick by brick. But wire anyway."

I retreated in good order and slept well. The next morning, the man in the beret appeared with a telegram in his hand and perplexity on his face. "She'll sell," he puzzled, and named a reasonable price.

But the greatest surprise was to find dozens of little adobes, near to mine and all along the hillside, filled with people whose names echoed musically in the ear—Escudero, Melendez, Trujillo. Truly, the Spanish thread had guided me home.

Of Sheep and Shepherds

Often in days gone by and occasionally even now, as a winter's night inks out the shining mesaland, one can see off against the encircling hills the faint glimmer of a campfire. By that fire sits one of the world's most solitary of men—a Spanish American shepherd.

As he waits and watches, alone under the low-hung New Mexico stars, little does he realize that he and his woolly animals have written an illumined page in American history.

For actually, sheep established New Mexico. They walked step by step with *conquistadores* and settlers over cactus-spiked deserts from Mexico to the almost mythical land of Cibola. When, in the 1590's, Oñate's settlers unloaded their scant belongings from squeaking *carretas* and dust-grey pack animals along the Rio Grande, there followed the sheep.

From that day, sheep fed and clothed the lonely dot of New Spain in the vast wilds of America. Harried by predatory Indians whose lands they had taken, sometimes almost forgotten by the mother country, separated by hundreds of dubious miles from their base of supplies in Mexico, the settlers had the sheep, a source of food and clothing in a wild and arid land.

The only transportation was by horse or mule. Woven into mantas or serapes, the surplus clip could be transported compactly down the long, Indian-haunted trail to Mexico. Yearly, many settlers went, or sent a substitute, with flintlock in crook of elbow down that trail on the *conducta* to the Chihuahua market. There the weaving of lost villages was traded for a few luxuries—a knife, a length of silk, the picture of a saint.

Shepherding foolish flocks from summer water

springs to sheltered valleys is lonely work. Weeks and months go by without much contact with other men. Of necessity, the shepherd sang as he sat by his little fire. From father to son, from shepherd to shepherd, the old plaintive songs have been handed down. Seventeenth-century Spanish ballads and lyrics broke the vast silences of what was to become an American state.

As the shepherds led their flocks in search of grass and water, they discovered in caves and along cliffs the footsteps of a long-forgotten people. Many are the stories the shepherds have told in the home village, of picture writing on great rocks, and of broken Indian pottery in lost arroyos.

The shepherd's little fire is only a pinprick of light against the black curtain of the encircling hills. He and dozens like him never dreamed that they established European civilization in primitive western America, that they speeded a romantic caravan of commerce, that they discovered an ancient Indian art, that they preserved the measures of prehistoric poetry, and that they stimulated the study of a people whose history was all unknown.

Rather, the shepherd thought of the snug little adobe house in his mountain village, where at Christmastime there was much dancing and merriment. He thought of the little Antonia and Pepe, who with the other children would be walking through the soft woollike snow to sing the Christmas songs of ancient Spain under little windows deep-set in thick adobe walls.

I wish he might have heard them, as I have, singing in the winter darkness the Spanish version of Holy Night:

> *Noche de paz,*
> *Noche de amor.*

Perhaps he heard another song under the Christmas stars in a land of tawny hills and humble, flat-roofed, little mud houses. There were other shepherds who did.

But aside from the beauty of the setting and the alluring, ancient folkways, it is the individual people of this high mesaland, the Apodacas and Cousin Canuto, the Indians like Cloud Eagle and Great-Grandmother Indian, and the Anglos like "Mees" Emily and "Mees" Boggers and all their ilk who make Christmas here a distinctive and heart-lifting experience.

Christmas in the Sky

My first Christmas in New Mexico was spent on the bleak, wind-swept top of barren Acoma. The four-hundred-foot-high mesa rises from a tableland, itself a mile above sea level. Even in summer it looks like an island of mystery, detached from the world in a shimmering ocean of wasteland.

Early in November we had eagerly accepted the invitation on our first visit there. María, daughter of the pueblo's governor, had urged us to keep

Christmas Day with them. But when the day came, it seemed a fantastic thing to do. We would have backed out if we could. People warned us that the Acomans, as a tribe, were not too friendly with visitors.

An icy wind was shrieking over the wasteland as we bumped along twenty miles of dirt road that led from the highway. Sand was blowing and dark scudding clouds gave the atmosphere a weird, green, ghostly tint. Reluctantly we left our car under a dwarf cedar tree at the base of the mesa and started up the winding sand trail to the pueblo that clings like a swallow's nest to the treeless summit.

Wind tore at our coats with icy fingers. Sand bit our faces with a thousand needle points and lodged in our watering eyes. At every step we sank ankle deep in sand. We kept thinking of Acoma's dramatic history, of house-to-house bloody battles and of Spanish soldiers who were hurled from the top down to the rocks below. There were stories of a Spanish priest who had disappeared into thin air and of an enormous rattlesnake cared for in a hidden cave by the tribe.

As we neared the top, the trail led through a wild welter of sandstone rocks carved by time and weather into brick-red, fantastic shapes. We jumped when something moved from the shadow of the overhanging cliffs on the summit. But it was only a little Indian girl with her mother's orange and green shawl fastened under her chin with a big safety pin.

She smiled and motioned us to follow her. But her companions were not so shy. All the small fry of Acoma formed a jabbering procession behind us as we bent before the wind, headed toward a group of terraced three-storied buildings. Lean hounds yelped and sniffed our ankles. Two lop-eared burros joined the hilarious procession brought up in the rear by a fierce-looking billy goat with a baleful gleam in his eye.

At last we stopped at one of the adobe and stone three-storied buildings built on the edge of the mesa. "María, she live on top house," instructed Shawl Girl and pointed calmly to a handmade ladder that led to the second floor. The ascent to the third looked even worse. Great cubical steps had been cut out of rock and adobe, evidently intended for giants. There was not even a handhold.

My friend shuddered, but rallied. "I can make it up," she gasped, "if I do it fast. But I know I can never get back down. I'll just have to join the tribe and spend the rest of my life up here."

María was standing in the doorway of her ancient penthouse. She was swathed to her eyebrows in a cherry-colored shawl. White doeskin boots reached to her knees, making her feet look absurdly small. "I hope you come," she smiled as she led the way into her skyey home.

On two sides, little windows looked out on illimitable horizons—shimmering wastelands below and cloud-scudding, jade-green sky above. The thick rock and adobe walls had been whitewashed until they glistened. A big iron cookstove winked a red eye. Along the sides of the room, ornate brass beds covered with handwoven blankets made comfortable seats, and a long table covered with a gay oilcloth was heaped with holiday fare.

There were towering pyramids of bread, brown-crusted and fragrant, fresh-baked in outside conical ovens. There was ceremonial bread, thin as tissue paper and looking like layers of blue wasp nest. There were mounds of beans and great bowls of lamb stew. Our offerings of candy, nuts, and fruit looked like pygmy fare among such lavish provision.

In one corner, a little piñon tree had been set up. It glittered with dime-store tinsel baubles just as our own at home did, but in addition it had been festooned with scarlet chile peppers and ears of blue and purple Indian corn. To its topmost branch had been wired three eagle feathers.

From the depths of the earth, somewhere outside, came the incessant pounding of ceremonial drums like the beat of waves against a subterranean shore. "We dance now in the church," María said, "the Butterfly Dance. Maybe you like to go."

Would we like to go! Ancient "pagan" Indian dances in a Catholic church hundreds of years old! María slipped down to the ground as easily as a beam of light. But how were we to get down those space-edged steps built for giants' legs? Indians had collected on surrounding rooftops. We solved the difficulty in a flash of inspiration. We simply sat down and bumped earthward to the accompanying whoops and yells of the assembled Acomans.

The old church, built like a fortress, was filled with shadows. Only a few little windows high in the massive walls let in an eerie light. A red-hot, pot-bellied stove and a few lighted candles scattered about the vast interior pricked the gloom.

Nearer and nearer came the pounding of the drums. Men and women dancers filed in. Chanters armed with rattle gourds huddled around the roaring drums. The women dancers gave a strangely oriental effect with crimson circles of paint on each brown cheek. Hair fresh-washed in amole root hung to their waists. Over their handwoven ceremonial dresses, they wore gorgeous shawls of blue, orange, and cerise satin. Their knee-high white boots twinkled. Around their necks and on their wrists and fingers they wore a glittering wealth of old silver and turquoise ornaments.

The men dancers, mostly bronze skin and dance kilt, also wore quantities of turquoise and silver. Fox skins dangled from lean hips, eagle and parrot feathers bobbed on blue-black heads. Sleigh

bells tinkled on rhythmic legs and arms. Ankles were twined with the sacred blue spruce.

Dancing, chanting, the pounding of drums, and the rattle of gourds went on hour after hour. Sweat poured from bronze bodies. Every step was precision and every tone perfect. They danced until approaching night came down over that sky-top mesa in modern America.

Suddenly, the dancing and chanting stopped. Came an almost tangible silence. The change was breathtaking. More and more candles were lighted on the black void of the altar. Indians in little groups moved toward the candlelight. There, highlighted in the darkness was a manger scene. On either side of it stood an Indian boy with a long rifle of ancient vintage. Their young faces were serious with the responsibility of protecting the Christ Child.

Toward the manger, the Indians of Acoma moved and left their Christmas offerings—strands of crimson chiles, ears of blue and purple corn, golden pumpkins, and their own beautiful pottery. There they heaped their dearest treasures—cans of milk and tomatoes, marshmallow-topped store cookies, and boxes of soda crackers.

Outside in the high bell tower, someone belabored the ancient bell. Its sounds mingled with the wind and with the whispering of piñon trees in the valley below. Wood smoke poured from fat adobe chimneys in the ruddy ancient buildings.

Dazed, we walked to the edge of the mesa where the sand trail led to our car—and another world. María and many of the pueblo people walked with us. "Stay tonight," they begged. "Stay all week. The priest who can visit us but once a year will be here in a day or two. There will be weddings and dancing and much feasting."

They filled our arms with strands of scarlet chiles and ears of Indian corn and a sample of their beautiful pottery. As we felt our way down the darkening trail, we could see the little group outlined against the winter sky. Neither they nor I knew at that time that they had given me a key to another world.

Little House with Wide Horizons

Now that the Little Adobe House and I have seen more than twenty Christmases together, I am thinking how much of my deep content originates in Tenorio Flat and its people. I bought my wedge of ruddy adobe earth and three little houses, never dreaming that in time I was to discover another whole new world to one side of me. In those days it was a little world of blue-hooded wells, dim lamplight by night and the pungent fragrance of piñon wood glowing in old iron stoves.

Spanish rolled around the little houses like a melodious sea.

Now, almost every little house has its own TV antenna, its radio, its piped water and gas, and its so-much-a-month *automóvil* or *troque*—truck. But Spanish labials still roll musically around the little houses.

For a long time, I had the only teléfono available to far-flung Tenorio Flat. Only a few others had come in through the years. There is seldom a day that my own is not borrowed. "Of course, you may borrow my teléfono," I tell Adolfo, who finds it necessary to talk with his girl on Agua Fria Street. The necessity arises several times a day. "But why don't you use the Vigil phone only a few steps from your own adobe? Why walk way up here?"

Adolfo looks at me with concern for my ignorance. "Those Vigil people have not the politeness," he shrugs. "Their folks did not come here from Chimayo or Truchas or Trampas back in *las montañas*. They come from down south in the state."

In the first days of my occupancy, I noticed many beshawled women passing down my driveway early in the morning. One day the housework procession halted, and a member who spoke some English addressed me. "Do we have the permeet to pass through your yard?" she queried. The procession stood rigid with concern that the new Anglo might abolish the short cut to their work.

"Of course," I nodded. They still pass. So do their menfolk, their schoolward bound children, their numerous canines, and even a pet rabbit or two.

I began reading New Mexico history, not for college credits, but for a clue to my neighbors. This led to their folklore and their arts. I had bought a New Mexico adobe and had acquired a far-flung, ever expanding kingdom.

In a few years, another kingdom was added: that of the local Indians. I had been reveling in Indian dances up and down the Rio Grande, but I knew little about Indians. I had even been up in the Navajo country and witnessed a Yei-be-chai far back in the mountains beyond Chinle. It was all beautiful beyond expression, but it remained a closed book.

It might have stayed that way, had not the head of the New Mexico Association on Indian Affairs, hurried into my adobe one day. By that time I was publishing a few Spanish background sketches in an eastern publication, but nothing about Indians.

"Will your paper publish anything about the Navajos?" she asked. "They are at their lowest ebb and we can get nothing about them into Eastern papers. After cutting down the number of sheep a Navajo family may graze, the Indian Bureau has put nothing in their place. Some of the tribe are literally digging up roots to make a kind of soup. Their tribal meeting comes up in a couple of weeks. Will you go with me to that week-long meeting and write something about it for an Eastern paper?"

I told her I knew little about Indians, especially the Navajos. She dashed home and returned with a mountain of books. I read day and night.

But reading is not seeing. The first night at Window Rock, in the large, attractive building in which government employees were housed, I retreated to my room on the second floor. It was equipped with every modern device of that time. But that steam-heated room was too warm. As I raised a window, I noticed something that caused me to turn out the lights and to draw up a chair to that window.

At a little distance, perhaps fifty Navajos, men, women and children, were sitting around a red-blazing, fragrant, cedar fire. Meager food was being passed from hand to hand, babies slept warmly wrapped in their mothers' arms. Older children played happily at a little distance among the cedar trees. There was much laughter. As children became weary, they were carried to nearby, white-covered wagons. When all was quiet, the men began to sing. They sang for hours the ancient songs of their people. I watched and listened in a kind of ecstasy. With all their poverty, they are happier than those non-Indians downstairs, I decided.

For almost a week I attended meetings with attendant Navajos and officials from Washington trying to explain the why and the wherefore. My report was published in an Eastern newspaper. But so far as I am concerned, that is the husk of the experience.

For years now, I have been trying to discover why both Navajo and Pueblo Indians seem happier than their so-called conquerors. That search has given me glimpses of a people whose philosophy is geared to harmony with the universe in which they live—both the tangible and the intangible. Only a few years ago, I heard a university-educated Pueblo Indian remark confidently, "When we dance for rain, it rains when we do it right and think right."

A Soldier Returns

Tío Antonio, the old one, sagged his stiff bones back in the sturdy chair he had made long years ago. A fire of piñon wood in the little corner fireplace cast a ruddy shadow on thick, whitewashed walls. Overhead, pine-tree ceiling beams glowed like old amber. Outside, where snow blanketed the New Mexico mesaland, the flat-roofed adobe houses of the remote village of Los Borregos looked like ruddy toys packed in cotton batting.

Beneath his wisps of white hair, Tío Antonio's

dark eyes twinkled. "So," he chuckled, "even on *Noche Buena*—Christmas Eve—our young *soldado* must be thinking of his machines. Since he has come home from being a fighting man in another World War he finds no happiness in his village. No? Machines our *soldado* must have, machines that roar, in place of sheep that baa."

Young Tonito teetered in his high-heeled, ranchman's boots toward the fire. A month ago, he had put aside his uniform with the overseas ribbon. It was good to be back in his bright blue levis, his cerise shirt, and silver concha belt. Even now, his hair was outgrowing the GI haircut. It hung down in black triangles in front of his ears. An embarrassed grin lighted his brown face. But his eyes were two black question marks.

"Me, I find out in army, I have good hands," he boasted. "I can feex anytheeng—jeeps, rahdios, beeg tanks. Has this village one thing I can feex? No! And the nearest electric juice, a hundred miles away."

Tío Antonio leaped from his chair. "Sí, we have machines in the village. Señora Archuleta has machine for the washing. It works weeth a steek she pulls back and forth. And Señora Melendez has machine for the sewing. I remember when her grandfather brought it by burro over the hills from Santa Fe. A wonder, that machine! and Señor Pino del Rio has *automóvil*. Ay, that it have no engine and is but a roost for the cheekens."

From the big iron cook stove at the other end of the room, Tía Lupita padded uneasily toward her old and young Antonio. "Peace we should have on *Noche Buena*," she begged. "The little fried pies burst themselves with piñon nuts. Eat and say if they hold spice enough." As her two men took huge bites and rolled approving eyes, she muttered, "If María Eufemia Valdéz were likewise out of uniform and back in the village, we would have no more talk of machines day and night."

"So," cackled Tío Antonio, "María Eufemia, a woman of wisdom, that one! Now that *la guerra*—the war—is over, María Eufemia will return to her village to stay. She plans, so she said on her last furlough, to make us all anti—anti—"

"Septic," shrugged Tonito. "It means without bugs."

"Sí, antiseptic!" his uncle shook with the quaint idea. "*Todo el mundo*—all the world—antiseptic, the water in the blue-hooded well, the corrals, the little ones! Sí, and even Tía Lupita!"

"Lady warriors I do not like," Tonito frowned,

remembering María Eufemia's unsatisfactory letters. Always she wrote of the village as if the big hospital where she worked did not exist.

He hurled himself into his great sheepskin coat and crammed his battered felt hat on his head. "I go now with the wood wagon to Tierra Roja to bring back our schoolmaster as you promised," he said coldly. "Perhaps we will stay for the Mass of the Cock's Crow." He paused at the blue-painted door to add with what he thought was dignity, "Before the war, okay, I was a shepherd. After the war, okay, I am a man of machines."

Tonito left the old man chuckling beside the fireplace. All the way along the twisting narrow road, the boy brooded until his face was as dark as the murky piñon trees that dotted the white hills. What a road! What poor little ranches! What houses made of mud! And not so much as a mousetrap in the way of a machine!

He stopped the horses on the edge of the purple mesa and looked down on Tierra Roja in the valley below. Usually Tierra Roja was just another village. In summer its sun-baked houses clung to a dusty plaza. In winter it slept under snow with only a silver feather of smoke blowing from each squat chimney to show there was life in the place. But tonight, it shimmered through the darkness like a spangled Christmas tree. *Las luminarias*—pyres of burning piñon wood—outlined its crooked narrow streets and central plaza. Even from up on the mesa, Tonito could smell the fragrance of wood smoke and see the resinous flames. On flat rooftops and on the twin belfries of the old church, *los farolitos*—paper-bag lanterns holding a lighted candle—twinkled and beckoned like low-hung stars.

For the first time since he had been home, he whistled as he walked along the snow-piled streets. The strum of guitars, the wail of a violin, and high-pitched children's voices came to his ears. He stepped aside in the snow to let a straggling procession pass. At its head walked a youthful Saint Joseph with his carpenter's tools on his back. He was leading a lop-eared burro on which was perched a small girl wrapped in a sky-blue shawl. She kept clutching at the tinsel crown that rested on her long black hair. Over the crown was a white veil. It floated straight out in the cold mountain breezes.

"*Las Posadas*," Tonito smiled. "Mary and Joseph trying to find room in an inn." Once he had been Saint Joseph and María Eufemia had been the Virgin. Kids had been acting that out for hundreds of years here in forgotten adobe villages.

He went smiling into the one-room school. The people were packed four-deep in old-fashioned, double-desk seats. Shrill whispers and smothered giggles came from behind the curtain screening one end of the room. *Los Pastores*—The Shepherds—should have been half-finished at least, but the old folk play had not started. In a minute, Tonito saw what was wrong. The kerosene lantern, high over the improvised stage, had refused to move on its guiding wire. The Star of Bethlehem was stuck in its course. Tonito felt in his pocket for the ever present pliers. Mounted on two chairs and a box, he straightened the kinked wire. The crowd clapped and whistled. "Hallo, Tonito! Welcome home, Tonito!"

Still the play did not go on. Neighbor told neighbor, "It is Miguel, archangel! He fell and hurt his leg. *Pobrecito*—poor little one! And no one knows his words!"

Like the lilt of an old song, the words came to Tonito. Tío Antonio had taught him. That was the way it had always been. No one took the trouble to write the words down. The old taught the young, words that had been passed on from one generation to another.

In two minutes Tonito was back of the ballooning curtain. In three, he had draped Miguel's purple mantle over his cerise shirt and blue levis. In four, the curtain parted to show the shepherds, their crooks twined with garlands of paper flowers, seated around their little fire. The kerosene lantern moved as a star should. The devil pranced and slithered in his wicked black tights. The hermit foiled him with the cross. The shepherds moved on with much singing to Bethlehem. Once again, right had triumphed over wrong.

Shepherds, hermit, devil, the angels of Heaven, followed by the villagers, hurried through the snow to an old church lost in a curtain of blackness. Soon a village boy in a lace-trimmed cotta, was lighting candles on the ancient altar. It was like being hurled from one world to another. From the high choir loft came the voices of village people singing the Spanish hymns of *Noche Buena*. And from a corner, Anglo cowboys buzzed with them like bumblebees.

As Tonito hurried out through the great door, he almost stumbled over a lady warrior—khaki overcoat, man's tie, and visored cap. "Tonito!" María Eufemia cried. "*Feliz Navidad*, Tonito."

"*Feliz Navidad*," replied Tonito, stiff as a pine

tree. But before he could become really dignified, the schoolmaster burst in upon them. He was a little man in a too big, dragging overcoat and he wore two hats. A knitted woolen cap, was pulled low over his ears against the cold. On top of this perched a low-crowned black felt at a matador's angle.

"Well met, Tonito," he gasped. "And María Eufemia, more lovely than ever! *Feliz Navidad!*"

Wrapped in fraying Chimayo blankets on the high seat of the old wood wagon, the three started back over the icy, twisting road. María Eufemia could not wait to see her village.

Down in a sheltered hollow a fire glowed. Sheep moved restlessly about. "A shepherd," nodded the schoolmaster. "Since the beginning of time one of the most important of people."

"What's so important about shepherds?" laughed Tonito.

"Sheep fed and clothed the little dots of New Spain," the schoolmaster said, "and in those dots, European culture began in a new world."

The door of Tío Antonio's house opened at the sound of wheels. Tía Lupita had been piling piñon logs in the corner fireplace.

"I love it!" María Eufemia danced up and down the room. "The sight of it! The smell of it! It's home!" She wiped away happy tears.

"What's new in Santa Fe?" Tío Antonio asked the schoolmaster when things had quieted down to bowls of hot chile and beans.

"Such news as you never heard," the little man exploded. "Good roads, hard roads, they are planning now that the war is over. Even to our little adobe village. Roads for *automóviles*. Ay, and electricity brought by singing wires. It is all planned."

Tonito choked over the rich hot chocolate spiced with cinnamon. "Machines! Machines for me to feex!"

"*Verdad*," shouted the schoolmaster. "*Automóviles* snorting up over the mesa and blowing up right in front of the fine garage . . ."

"Of Tonito, the best auto mechanic een all New Mexico," laughed María Eufemia.

Excitement along the Deetch

Ever since Christmas night, snow had been falling at intervals over our thirsty rosy land. From mountain heights to vast rock-rimmed valleys, all was a sea of whiteness. Even along the driveway to my small adobe, snow was over a foot deep. It was a hushed time for nightly fireplace enjoyment and almost tangible quiet.

But one night about nine o'clock, the violinist in my front adobe telephoned in some excitement. "There's a truck in the ditch along the front of the lot. The driver is an elderly Spanish American who can't speak much English. The license plate shows he is from Rio Arriba County way up north. He's evidently a stranger here and completely lost. When he realized he was in a dead-end street, he probably tried to turn around on your parking area and slid into the ditch. His two back wheels are stuck to their hubs in adobe. His two front wheels are on terra firma. His engine sounds all right, but it can't move those rear wheels."

"I'll bundle up and be right out," I promised.

By the light of our two flashlights, we observed the ancient truck with its rear tilting perilously toward the adobe-gripped rear wheels. The owner greeted us with smiles and a cascade of Spanish. By signs he indicated that he would sleep in the truck all night. He evidently would not trust that precious vehicle to possible vandals of our big city—snow or more snow.

"He probably hasn't a drop of antifreeze in that engine and his clothing is thin and old. We can't let him sit there all night. It's well below zero now," decided the violinist.

But how to convince him with our limited Spanish! And then I heard someone singing as he plowed through the white drifts back of us. It was

45

Cousin Canuto, swathed like a mummy, returning from town. He took one look at the old man in the truck and exclaimed, "It's Abuelo—Grandfather—Casados from a ranchito in the county of Rio Arriba."

The two men exchanged greetings and inquired about the health of each other's families in

unhurried detail. Cousin Canuto then invited the little old man to come to his casita for the night.

With thanks, with a million of thanks, the kind invitation was declined. Abuelo Casados would not desert his truck. All he wanted was to go home to the county of Rio Arriba—"weeth *troque.*"

The violinist motioned us aside. "We will have to call the police. Maybe they can get that truck out of the ditch. But if they do, they mustn't let that old man head for Rio Arriba County. He would find himself in a mountain of snow."

Cousin Canuto and the violinist disappeared into her adobe and had scarcely rejoined me when a police car with a huge floodlight rolled onto the snow-filled lot. Out sprang a Spanish American policeman. Spanish flowed like the surge of the sea. Right behind this police car came another, also floodlighted. Out jumped another Spanish American policeman. Spanish flowed like the meeting of the seven seas.

The two policemen and Cousin Canuto pulled from the front and pushed from the back. But the truck sank only more deeply into ice-coated, frozen adobe. More Spanish flowed in staccato on the frozen air. "We'll have to send for a wrecker," decided the police. Another trip was made to the violinist's telephone. In no time, up rolled a huge wrecker manned by two more Spanish Americans. Spanish flowed again in mounting crescendo. Just behind the wrecker came a third police car also floodlighted. It was manned by a Spanish American policeman. Spanish flowed like the ultimate deluge.

But the wrecker did the work. The truck returned to terra firma. The engine ran smoothly. All was well. Cousin Canuto, the wrecker crew, three policemen, the violinist, and I held a hurried council of strategy, out of earshot of the still calm but persistent abuelo.

"That old man says all he wants now is to drive his *troque* home to the county of Rio Arriba," explained Cousin Canuto. "I asked him to come to my home, but he would not. You know what could happen."

The three policemen nodded their heads. "Put his truck under cover somewhere. And put him in the city jail where he can't get out to find it."

"We'd have to give the officer at the desk some reason for holding him," said the senior police.

"Reason enough," blustered one of the wrecker crew. "Disorderly conduct. Look at the Señora's fence. Flat in the ditch! And all of us here in below-zero weather trying to get his truck out."

"That was an accident," decided Cousin Canuto. "Just tell the officer in charge it is to preserve life and limb—his own and anyone else's on the road to the County of Rio Arriba."

"We'll do it," shouted the senior officer. "The road should be safe in a day or two."

At this, the procession re-formed and rolled into the snow-packed street. First came one police car with floodlight glowing in the dark night. Then came the ancient truck guided by an equally ancient abuelo. Came the second floodlighted police car, followed by the cumbersome wrecker with its two attendants, and finally the third police car, also floodlighted. All moved to the melody of shrilling sirens.

In all, that little episode made quite a procession through the dark night—one elderly Spanish American, three policemen, two wrecking-crew experts, and Cousin Canuto—six good men and true to keep one elderly abuelo from going home over the frozen drifts to the County of Rio Arriba.

Christmas as Old as Time

An Indian Christmas is not an easy expedition. It seems easy enough when we plan it in summer with the sun pouring down warmly on adobe walls of ancient pueblos, with the sluggish Rio Grande chuckling by under the gnarled, leafy cottonwood trees, and the pueblo dwellers bringing in the harvest of blue and purple corn and scarlet chile.

This part of northern New Mexico usually sees

a white Christmas. The wind whoops it up with wild cowboy yells through the high mountain passes. Off the main highways, the whole region suddenly becomes a white labyrinth of tangled, snow-buried, dirt roads.

We who live here are hounds for punishment. As we turn up the thermostat in our snug adobe houses and toss a couple of piñon chunks into our corner fireplaces, we plan to be sensible for once and stay comfortably at home. But we know in the bottom of our hearts we will not. We are completely bewitched by the memory of booming Indian drums.

Indian Christmas comes in to the roar of drums instead of to the peal of bells. In Taos, if the wind is right, people can stay comfortably in bed and hear the growl of rawhide drums across the snowy hills. But the rest of us have to travel miles to hear that strange Christmas sound.

About eight o'clock on Christmas Eve, when we should be wrapping something in the way of a belated gift for Aunt Melora, or stuffing the Christmas turkey, we give in. We put on layers of our warmest clothes, chains are put on the tires, and we start. From then on, we are decidedly bewitched, and we know from many experiences that we won't be back to normal for months—if ever. It's the memory of those drums.

The night is deep indigo blue sagging with stars overhead. The minute we leave the highway, we lose all sense of direction in the snow-drifted maze. Dirt roads, that in summer were as familiar as our own dooryards, become mysterious. We argue if we turn at the third or fourth bridge to reach Cochiti. We might as well save our frosty breath because there are no bridges to be seen anywhere. We wander around in a vast uncharted wilderness of snow and finally, to our surprise, find ourselves slap against the round sides of an Indian kiva. We remember that Whites are not supposed to approach this ancient seat of Indian religion. We women squirm as we remember that snakes are supposed to be kept in underground hiding-places of these kivas. We suspect that is just a tall tale, but we squirm.

We back gingerly away and park vaguely at a respectable distance. Calmed, we make out the dim shapes of clustered adobe houses around a central plaza and the darker shadow of an old Franciscan church. A few paper bags with lighted candles within them dot the roof tops. Otherwise, no one seems to live here. Someone thinks this is not Cochiti, but we decide to remain anyway. We feel lucky to have found any pueblo.

When we get out of the car, a blast from icy mountaintops hits us and we stumble along on legs so cold and stiff that we seem to be walking on stilts. Dogs growl and sniff our heels. Horses and cattle mill around in corrals. Sheep baa and that sets all the dogs to howling.

We make a dash for the black shadow that is the old church. It takes our united efforts to open the ponderous hand-carved door. It is almost as dark inside. A few frail islands of light flicker along whitewashed walls where candles burn in tin holders. We are out of the freezing wind now, but it seems colder inside—a dank cold of musty, three-foot-thick adobe walls and unaired space. A corpulent iron stove burns in the center of things. It gives out a delicious fragrance of piñon wood, but it doesn't seem to give much warmth for all its glowing.

We knew when we started that we probably would have to stand up for hours. No softly cushioned pews in this church! We find a section of adobe wall that seems to be empty and we lean against it. Up and down the dank walls we dimly make out the forms of other resigned leaners. Within a half hour, the marrow of our bones is congealed.

Nothing at all happens. We lean and we congeal, and we manage to take in the beautiful proportions of the old church—its tree-trunk ceiling beams upheld by carved wooden corbels; its dim, very Spanish pictures of the saints whose muted faces manage to express exalted emotions.

When we are about to give the whole thing up and make a dash for home, if we can find our car, which is doubtful, we catch the sound we have been waiting a year to hear again. The muffled beat of Indian drums! That beat starts in the underground kiva, it crosses the snowy plaza and comes nearer and nearer. We have heard that pom-pom of rawhide drums dozens of times, but we feel prickles run up and down our spines.

Chanters follow the drums. They bob up and down to the rhythm. Dancers file in and soon the pebble-wash of rattle gourds and the jingle of bells on prancing legs mingles with the pat-pat of feet and the never ceasing growl of the drums.

A few more candles are lighted. The men dancers are wearing the handsome, handwoven, black kirtle decorated with symbols of red, green, and other colors. On their feet, they wear deerskin moccasins, some topped with skunk fur to keep evil spirits away. Fox skins trail from waist to heel and fly wildly out behind as the dancing gains in tempo. Elbows and knees are bound with blue spruce twigs, symbol of everlasting life. Green and yellow parrot feathers bob on heads, even if they are wired to a GI haircut. Chains of uncut turquoise, coral, and strings of shells sway on bronze chests. So strenuous is the dance that soon the dancers are sweating and we rather envy them.

Women dancers wear the handwoven, knee-length, manta that fastens on one shoulder and leaves the other bare. High, white, deerskin boots twinkle in the half-light. Back shawls of scarlet, orange, and bright blue satin float in the dank air. They, too, wear a wealth of turquoise, coral, and fine old silver jewelry. In either hand they carry bunches of evergreen, and most of their dancing is done with expressive hand and arm movements. Their feet simply follow the pattern of the men's more active movements.

Hour after hour the dancing continues. Soon we are so absorbed by it that we are conscious only of moving color—spirals and arcs and planes of crimson, bronze, purple, and blue, with the glint of candlelight focused on a silver bracelet or a polished abalone shell.

The chanting rises and falls with a spirited pantomime of gestures. It almost dies out. It starts again with renewed fervor. It has perfect tempo and rhythm. A saturation of odors presses upon us—musty walls, ancient worm-eaten timbers, candle grease, stale incense, crushed spruce branches, woolen clothing, and sweat.

The drums never stop. Toward the last, it seems as if the yard-thick adobe walls must buckle and fall, that the roof must sail off into indigo space, and drummers, chanters, and dancers disappear in the Christmas sky.

But they do not. Suddenly comes a great quiet that beats on the ears. A little Indian in a red cassock lights dozens of candles on the old high altar. As suddenly as the Franciscans appeared along the Rio Grande four centuries ago, the Indians turn to Christian rites. They drop to their knees for the midnight mass.

Some of the women climb the steep steps to the choir loft in the rear. On its plank railing, they place lighted candles. They sit wrapped in their red, orange, and plum-colored shawls. Babies sleep in their arms. In their high, reedy voices, Indian women sing the old liturgical music of the church. History has flipped a page so suddenly that we are left stunned and breathless.

If we ask a young Indian why they are dancing in the ancient church on Christmas Eve, he will answer, "We dance to honor the Christ Child." But the incessant pounding of drums, the mono-syllabic chanting, the stamping feet, the convolutions of raw pigment, add up to something far more primitive and earthy. Deep down within us we have sensed a glimmer of what that something is. It is earth and sky and the winds that blew between the stars when the human race was young.

The Pueblo Indians accepted to some degree the religion the friars brought them. They have kept it all these years in a certain compartment of their minds and hearts. But their own traditions of earth, sky, rain, and sun they have also kept.

It just happens that the winter solstice falls close to Christmas Day. That is the time when Earth Mother stretches and yawns and gives a little push toward longer days, sunnier skies, spring rains, and seed-planting time. The dancing and drum-pounding is to usher her on her way. If at the same time they can honor the Christ in the Manger, so much the better. But of late years, the order of ceremonies has been changed with the Christian mass coming first and the Indian ceremonial dancing last.

Someway our frozen bones function enough to get us back to the car. It has not disappeared down the ladder-hole in the kiva as seemed probable when the drum-pounding was at its height. Right in the midst of our own Christmas, we hear the roll of Indian drums. It all happened a thousand miles away, a thousand years ago.

Horn of Many Thunders

Mees Emily's Indian friend, Cloud Eagle, takes care of her walled patio where white lilies bloom and white pigeons spread soaring wings. Cloud Eagle lives far down the Rio Grande in a pueblo back from the highway. Mees Emily has no way of summoning him when she needs his help. But always he appears when work needs to be done. "I think you need me today," he says. "I come."

One day he appeared at her door in late morning when she did not need him at all. But, according to custom, she prepared the lunch which they always eat together. After lunch her guitar was brought out, also according to custom, and they sang together the ancient Indian songs he had taught her through the years. If she forgot a single word in a song, they sang it over and over until it was perfect. Cloud Eagle is a stickler for perfection of word and rhythm.

After the music lesson in ancient Indian syllables, Cloud Eagle settled back in his chair to explain his presence in Santa Fe when no garden work was needed. "Is long walk from my pueblo to highway. Then is long walk to your house. At night, I have to do it all over again. Sometimes, Indian who marry my daughter, Little Pink Flower, let me take his wagon that flies. But not often. So I save and save money. Now I can buy wagon that flies. I go now to buy old wagon that flies."

Mees Emily had to think fast. She had heard how some secondhand car dealers took advantage of old Indians who did not know much about what made wagons fly.

"Cloud Eagle," she ventured, "all the many years you know me, I drive wagon that flies, myself, even into the big land of the Navajos. When I live on rancho, far from Santa Fe, I have to make little repairs and change the tire. I have to. Let's make a feast day! Let me go with you when you buy your wagon that flies."

Cloud Eagle smiled with the wisdom of the old-time Indian. "Today you do not need me. I need you."

Soon Mees Emily, in full Navajo costume set off by a discreet selection of her silver and turquoise jewelry, seated herself in her car. Beside her sat Cloud Eagle upright as a yellow pine. His arms were crossed in statuesque pose over his chest. From time to time he reached over and tooted the horn to aid progress.

On the used car lot operated by an acquaintance, Mees Emily inspected every car within Cloud Eagle's price range. Only one seemed possible from engine to tires. Cloud Eagle paid little attention. He had seated himself in an ancient number that had little to recommend it, either in inner working or outward tires. There he sat on the tattered upholstery, tooting the old-fashioned bright brass horn worked by a rubber bulb. "Listen, listen," he demanded. "The horn of many thunders."

"That wagon that flies is no good," pleaded Mees Emily. "Listen to the engine and get out and see how thin are the tires. You must not buy that car."

But Cloud Eagle sat with rapture on his face as he tooted the shining horn of the car of his dreams. He would not look at another.

Finally the proprietor, in sheer desperation, suggested that the horn of many thunders might be installed on the car Mees Emily had approved. He called his workmen and, after some delay, Cloud Eagle drove off the lot announcing his passage with the horn of many thunders.

Within a week, Cloud Eagle was back in Mees Emily's patio. He had walked all the way from his pueblo. Why had he not driven his fine wagon that flies?

"I have to answer questions and get a little card," groaned Cloud Eagle. "I have only three years in Indian Bureau day school long, long ago." Cloud Eagle groaned again. "Maybe I cannot get little card so I can drive wagon that flies."

"Of course you have to answer questions to get a driver's license," groaned Mees Emily. "I thought you had one. You often drove your son-in-law's car."

"The Indian who marry my daughter, Little

Pink Flower, have his card. I think that is enough for all the family."

Day after day, Mees Emily coached Cloud Eagle in the proper answers to all questions appertaining to the skippering of a secondhand car over the highways of the state.

But Cloud Eagle flunked the examination. He flunked miserably, but they would give him another chance.

Followed more days of questions and stumbling replies by Cloud Eagle. If the examiner only spoke Tewa! But Cloud Eagle flunked this examination more miserably than the first. He would have to walk back and forth to Santa Fe, even if he owned a wagon that flies.

When Mees Emily's patio and borders needed to be put to bed for the winter, Cloud Eagle appeared at her gate in a taxi. "I think you need me," he announced. "I take bus to Santa Fe and take taxi to your house. Will do same thing when I go home."

"But that will take all you earn," groaned Mees Emily.

"I make lots of money," laughed Cloud Eagle. "All the young Indians want to rent my wagon that flies and its shining horn. When is feast day at

Acoma or Old Laguna or Jemez, all those young Indians want to rent my wagon that flies. They fight to get it."

"Nights at home," whispered Cloud Eagle, "I drive wagon that flies around and around dance plaza. I listen to the horn of many thunders. People stand in open doors to hear. They clap, they shout the greeting. That shining horn gives off sparks of fire like moonbeam on snowy Truchas Peak. Now where you want to put lily bulbs?"

The New Sewing Machine

When yellow roses of Castille encircled the adobe house like a golden necklace, Carmencita came bursting into it like a winter wind, "I never think that my mamacita would do such a thing," she exclaimed. "Five years she has been fooling my papá!"

"Come, come, Carmencita," I reasoned, "you can't expect me to believe that. Start at the beginning and tell me what happened, if you think papá and mamá would not mind."

"All Tenorio Flat knows and is laughing," she wept. "You remember five Christmases ago when papá gave mamacita a new electric sewing machine to take the place of that funny old one worked by a foot treadle? That clumsy old machine had made all our baby clothes and mamacita kept right on using it to make her own clothes, and housedresses for Lupe and Luz, and things for all the grandchildren and friends and neighbors."

I had often wondered how she found time to do all that sewing in between her own housekeeping and helping Miss Boggers and Miss Emily.

At that point, came a knock at the door and Mrs. Apodaca, eyes flashing, burst into the room. "Carmencita, I weel tale the story of the new sewing machine myself," she announced.

Settled in the big rocker, she explained, "I try to like that new *máquina* that sews and that papá geeve me five Chreesmases ago. My hands and feet and my eyes had worked so many, many years weeth old *máquina* that weeth new one, they do all the wrong theengs. I do not want to hurt the feelings of papá. I try long time and spoil much good cloth. Besides the old *máquina*, papa pay out much *dinero* to geeve me the new one.

"Do not look at me weeth deesdain, Carmen-cita. I have much sewing to do for Lupe and Luz and all the grandchildren and the leetle half-orphans and Grandma Segura out een Pecos village. That new *máquina* and I do not get along together. But I do not tale papá. I do not want to hurt the feelings of papá."

"So you take all the things you want to sew to Cousin Canuto's house and use María Lupita's old, old sewing machine and to Grandma Casado's house way down on Agua Fria Street and a lot of other places wherever you can find an old wreck of a machine. And then you come home and pile all the things you have made on the new machine papá thinks you are using," Carmencita said.

With just the trace of a twinkle in her troubled eyes, Mrs. Apodaca confessed that papá looked at all the sewing and said, "See how many more nize theengs you can make weeth new *máquina*. More and better than you ever made weeth old *máquina*."

"You mean that for five years, in winter snow and summer sun, you have been walking miles to do your sewing?" I gasped.

"Sí, Senora. Eet was hard. But I deed not want to hurt the feelings of papá. But weeth Mees Boggers geeving more and beeger parties and Mees Emily wanting me to help her, I have to say to myself that I cannot keep on like thees. I do not know what to do. I am een deespair."

Mrs. Apodaca wiped her eyes and smiled. "But one day I see a stranger man een leetle *troque* going from house to house een the Flat. I cannot believe my eyes. Een back of *troque* ees an old *máquina* that look just like my old one. I run up close to see and man say, "I just sold fine new *máquina* electrica to Spanish lady een Truchas and take thees old *máquina* as part of down payment een cash. Could I eentress you een fine new *máquina* electrica?"

"I say, 'You cannot, but please breeng that old *máquina* eento my casita and let me try eet.' Señora, that old *máquina* run just like my old one. My hands and my eyes know what to do weethout theenking. I am very excite. I say, 'Weel you trade thees new *máquina* for the old one?'

"He look at me funny and I poot my name on paper he ask me to sign. Then he poot my new *máquina* een *troque* and leave old *máquina* een my house. Señora, I sew all day. My feet almost dance working el treadle."

"And papá comes home and finds the new machine gone and that old one in its place," added Carmencita. "Mamá have to tell him that she traded his Christmas gift of expensive new sewing machine for that funny old thing that you work with your feet."

"Was papá cross?" I asked, thinking that almost any man might be.

"No," confessed Carmencita, bewildered by the outcome. "He said mamacita had done just

69

right. He said every man liked an old hammer or saw that fitted his hand. He would not trade for a dozen new ones. He said mamacita was like that with her old sewing machine. She and that sewing machine knew each other. He should have known better."

Mrs. Apodaca nodded, smiled and said, "Now that I do not have to walk so far to use a *máquina* I can run, I weel make papá some fine summer shirts and next winter I weel make heem a nize warm robe of the bathing to wear on cold nights when he seet up to read Spanish-language newspaper."

But Carmencita still persisted. "Mamacita did not tell papá the truth for five years."

"I deed not want to hurt hees feelings," insisted Mrs. Apodaca.

Luminarias and Farolitos

Christmas in Santa Fe is unlike that in other cities of the nation. The emphasis is on the religious significance of the season expressed in a way that people of various beliefs and customs can accept and with which they can identify themselves.

The setting of the old town provides a natural backdrop of great forests high against a winter-blue sky. They shimmer with crystalline snow by day and are decorated by stars by night. World travelers remark that this setting of starry heights and color-dyed desert lands is very similar to that of the first Christmas.

Christmas here announces itself with a distinctive, delectable fragrance permeating the folds of the old town. It comes from burning piñon wood in countless fireplaces, both small corner ones and huge modern affairs. In the old days, little fires of piñon wood laid up crisscross on the ground were lighted on Christmas Eve. Originally three in number, they represented the Holy Family. Inside, a front window glowed with three lighted candles for the same reason. Even today one catches the scent of the little outside fires burning here and there along the old crooked streets. *Las luminarias*, everyone exclaims, drawing in great breaths of the nostalgic fragrance.

All over town, from the state government buildings on one side to the Governor's home on an opposite hilltop, from great hotels to tiny, crumbling adobe houses on forgotten byways, shine thousands of saffron-colored paper-bag lanterns with lighted candles within. *Los farolitos*, they are called, the little lanterns. Paper bags are a fairly recent institution, but the parchmentlike little lanterns had a forerunner in the early days of Spanish colonization.

According to Ina Sizer Cassidy, an authority on local tradition, the early Spanish colonists, long before the advent of the paper bag, lighted their rooftops with little fagots of pitch pine saved from their winter supply of wood. As roofs of adobe houses in those days consisted of a foot or so of hard-packed adobe supported by sturdy pine beams inside, there was little danger of fire from the blazing fagots along the roof edge.

From that beginning came the soft-hued, paper-bag lanterns. How their use has multiplied and spread even outside the state! Metropolitan Albuquerque has paper lanterns outlining its driveways, its walls and garden walks, as well as on its rooftops. Visitors in Santa Fe have not only transplanted the custom to Cape Cod cottages in New England, but to Oklahoma, Texas, California, and the Middle West.

The Old Santa Fe Association offers prizes each Christmas for homes decorated after the old manner with *luminarias* and *farolitos*. One of the most delightful customs of the season is to ride slowly at night from street to street and from dirt road to dirt road, taking in the scent of burning fires and the etching of paper-bag lanterns against the wintry sky.

One finds oneself on dark streets one never knew existed. One runs into small adobe houses where Christmas scenes have been painted in color on front windows by skillful native fingers. Even the state buildings look like tapestry against the winter sky. It is like riding about in a dream city with all the old beauties and ancient customs bursting into bloom for the greatest of days.

The Beeg, Beeg Star

Late in November one year, I received a gift. It is a sizable gift, being twelve miles of the most beautiful canyon I have ever seen in this New Mexico land of breathtaking chasms. I hold no deed on flimsy paper for that canyon. It is too vast a gift for such puny procedure. Attached to this bounty was a living Christmas card—real sheep and two dark-faced shepherds on a windy hilltop under a wintry sky.

As is often the case with good gifts, this one

came as a complete surprise. We were taking one last look at the Valley of the Cousins before winter set in. Clouds heavy with promised snow moved like cargo-heavy galleons across a milky sky. Suddenly we came to a wisp of dirt road we had never noticed before in all the years we had wandered up and down the valley.

The car practically turned itself into the narrow dirt road. Almost immediately we were in an enchanted place. It was wild uninhabited country with a little jade-green river moving languidly through the wide meadowland and high-walled gorges. Headlands like the fingers of a giant's hand jutted into wider spaces as if reaching for that somnolent stream. The sides, the summits of all the encircling walls and headlands were carved in the likeness of fabulous creatures there to guard palaces, courtyards, and temples.

But that stone was not gray. It was all the shades of fuchsia with touches of yellow, ivory, and verdigris. They were solidified color and light.

At the end of twelve miles, the wisp of road was almost blocked by the base of a soaring mesa also done in fuchsia shades. Its vertical sides mounted almost without break to a ruler-straight summit that seemed to touch the sky. What little was left of the road was crossed by a sturdy plank gate heavily chained and padlocked. Evidently the owner of this part of the canyon had his deed recorded.

On the other side of the river was a weather-beaten ranch house, the first habitation we had noticed. There was no way to get to it without crossing the river. Even a ranch house here had its moat, we decided. A rowboat, big and sturdy enough to cross the Father of Waters, was tied to a cottonwood tree on the road side of the river. We did not attempt to row ourselves across. No smoke was blowing from the ranch house chimney. We decided that the owners had left for the season. It will always remain a house of mystery in the shadow of the red and purple mesa.

When we returned to the road in the Valley of the Cousins, night was falling. Lazy snowflakes drifted with the wind. It was there that we saw the living Christmas card. On a bleak open space, we saw a flock of sheep being shepherded toward overhanging cliffs by two native *pastores*. From the fine appearance of the flock and the tattered condition of the shepherds, we surmised that they had been out many months in some alpine valley of the mountains. The shepherds were thin and hungry-looking. Their hair hung to their shoulders from under the torn brims of their sombreros. Their clothing was in rags. With them was a mouse-grey team of burros laden with wooden water kegs, a box for provisions, and rolls of ragged bedding.

But when we stopped, they gave us the flash of white teeth and the glow of happy eyes. "Sí, we have been far back in *las montañas*. Such grass! So green, so tender! Not one sheep lost! Not one! Look at the size of them, and the fleece! Ah, that fleece! Tonight we camp in the shelter of great cliffs. To-morrow we all be home."

"But snow could fall tonight," we protested. "Tomorrow you may not be able to get the sheep through the snow."

Los pastores laughed with delight at our lack of weather wisdom. "The wind blow the clouds toward the high snowy *montañas* where we were. *Mira, mira*—look, look—a beeg, beeg star up there."

We left them building a little fire of cedar wood in the shelter of the great rocks. As we looked back we could see its yellow light through the murky night. It seemed an earthly reflection of that beeg, beeg star up in the wintry sky.

I am finding that the gift of a canyon filled with color and light and its attendant card of shep-herds and sheep is giving a new depth and loveliness to the dear familiars of our regional Christmas season.

When people from the Spanish villages rattle into town in horse-drawn wagon or rickety truck, I scan each face hoping to see the shepherds. Perhaps I cannot recognize them with wild locks cut and under new sombreros. But I smile at them all with a new interest. People who can look beyond wind-blown clouds and see a star, are part of Christmas.

My own corner fireplace with its purring flames has become a campfire in the shadow of a great rock. I, too, can look through my deep-set window and see a beeg, beeg star.

Great-Grandmother Wins

Quite suddenly, Great-Grandmother startled her daughter by suggesting that they all go to the Albuquerque fair. Elderly Pueblo Indian women do not suggest such junketings. But the grandson, his wife, the two little children, the middle-aged daughter and her husband decided to humor her. She had many, many years. They would all go to the great fair which not one of them had ever seen.

If Great-Grandmother had never attended the

fair, her beautiful pottery had represented her. She had often won second and third prize ribbons. But of late years her daughter had thought that her mother's skill was declining. She had urged that she send no more entries.

The daughter and the granddaughter packed a huge old suitcase full of bowls, vases, and platters made by their pueblo potters. They also packed a large box with turquoise and silver jewelry. They were for sale, not for exhibit. Perhaps they might sell some and thus add to tribal income.

They had to walk a mile from the pueblo to the highway where they took a little bus to Santa Fe there to catch a big bus for Albuquerque. As they dropped down to lower elevations, the mesa-rimmed desertland shimmered with heat. Albuquerque was even hotter. They wandered around a full hour before they could find another bus to reach the fairgrounds. Flags and pennants on the huge fair buildings hung limp and lifeless in the heat.

The attendant at the door demanded admission tickets, but suggested that they might spread their tribal pottery and jewelry on a blanket outside the building where thousands of visitors milled about in a furnace of sunlight.

At the look of dismay on Great-Grandmother's

face and the whimpering of tired children, son-in-law and grandson held a whispered conference and announced that they would leave them for a little while. At the end of a blistering hour, they returned in the highest of spirits and led the drooping family to rooms they had found in a small motel. There was even a kitchen.

Inside it was cool as a cave. "Air conditioned," exulted the son-in-law, as he headed for a nearby shopping center from which he returned with boxes and bags of groceries. Then the women folk went into action, frying bacon, browning pancakes, and filling cups with cool milk. What a feast that was after all the sun-scorched miles! Then everyone calmly went to sleep until nightfall, when it seemed that another meal was in order.

Later, the two men strolled away and came back with exciting news. No, they had not been to the fair. They would stay in the cool little motel. But the next afternoon there was to be a baseball game by fellows who made baseball their business.

At this, Great-Grandmother, who seldom missed a pueblo game, assumed her proper place in the family circle. They would all go to see that game, she announced. They all went to sleep again and awakened with just time for a copious breakfast-lunch eaten to the tune of much laughter and chatter in their native Tewa.

Seated in the huge bleachers, Great-Grandmother, after much scrutiny, decided that the pitcher for one of the teams looked like an Indian and his team would win. She was too much of the old school to whoop and cheer like the white women, but her eyes shone like desert stars and at crucial points she patted her small brown hands together as gently as butterfly wings.

The team of the supposed Indian pitcher won by an impressive margin, to the delighted howls of the multitude. Great-Grandmother moved in a rapturous trance back to the air conditioned motel, to the Albuquerque bus station, to the bus that would carry them back to Santa Fe. There, carrying children who had never seen the fair, with heavy burdens of pottery and silver jewelry that had never been offered for sale, they learned that they had just missed the last small bus that would have taken them within a mile of their pueblo.

They sat happily in the Santa Fe bus station chatting of the cool motel, of the good beds, of the fine meals they had cooked, and the marvel of the first professional baseball game they had ever seen. As midnight approached and the children tossed in fitful sleep, Great-Grandmother rallied to her responsibilities. "Tall Pine," she urged, "call governor of our pueblo on wire that talks. Tell him to send someone with truck to take us and the pueblo pottery and jewelry home. Tell him we are summer-kiva people and to send a man who belongs to our summer-kiva people. Then we won't have to pay him anything."

In about an hour, Deer Go Lightly appeared to drive them home under the morning stars. Great-Grandmother sat on the front seat by Deer Go Lightly and regaled him with highlights of the baseball game and the pitcher of the winning team who, most certainly, was "of the people."

Back in the cool adobe house beside the ancient plaza, Great-Grandmother's daughter was feeling happy. She had saved her mother from the pain of not receiving a ribbon award for pottery she might have sent to the fair. She had seen her first big ball game and the pitcher who looked like an Indian, even if his name on the program spelled out Patsy O'Brien.

In came a pueblo woman who had not gone to the fair. "It was good Great-Grandmother got first and second prize for two bowls she sent to the fair. She never had a first before."

"But she did not send any bowls this year."

"She did send bowls—one big one, one little one. I wrap them up myself and I take them to Santa Fe to go express. Our pueblo governor go to the fair and bring back two ribbons for her. The little bowl get first prize and the big bowl get second. Here they are. Take them to her and tell her the pueblo is proud."

Knee-Deep in Padillas

It took many years of living in New Mexico to realize that, aside from the traditional facets of Christmas participated in by three divergent peoples, the real essence was found in the people themselves. It was the everyday human living of us all that made such a Christmas possible.

There was the day when I became bogged down in Padillas. It was late in May when the little adobe houses and encircling adobe walls were all restored to their pristine condition after winter snows. Julio, the old adobe maestro, with his helper, and Adolfo, the firewall expert, and his helper, had departed after all the customary amenities had been fulfilled.

Only one hurdle remained for me—*tierra*— red adobe earth. Piles of it filled the yard—discarded earth from disintegrated firewalls, heaps of it washed down from the hills. Where could I find a man with a big truck to remove this evidence of disorder? Every workman I knew "weeth *troque*" was booked weeks and months ahead.

In despair, I settled down in my writing-room to my own neglected work. I tried to forget those heaps of red earth defacing my small kingdom.

Came a timid knock at the writing-room door. There stood an elderly Spanish-speaking man, hat in hand. He spoke little English, but produced a cheap card printed in English. At the top was the euphonious name, Polito Padilla, with his street address and telephone number. Underneath was a list of useful things Polito could do. He could build with cement and adobe. He was a roofer. He was a cabinet-maker and could make regional furniture. At the end was a notation, *"Tierra* hauled away."

I told the dispenser of assorted services that I would call him at his home that evening. There were quite a few words I needed to look up in my Spanish dictionary before I entered into any agreement. The exigencies of *tierra* demanded a more copious vocabulary.

After dinner, I called the number on the little card. A voice answered and, at my question, insisted that it belonged to Polito Padilla. But the voice was not that of the man who had given me the cryptic card. It was the voice of a younger man, and I did not need to call upon my hastily acquired technical vocabulary. "Yes, yes, I am Polito Padilla. Yes, I haul *tierra* away een *troque*." When could he haul it away? "Oh, een a day or two."

After two weeks when no truck appeared, I called again.

"Sí, sí, Polito Padilla." But this voice was not like either of the other two Padilla men to whom I had talked. But they would come next day early in the morning to haul the *tierra* away.

At nine next morning appeared a young man who spoke English in the vernacular. "You bet, my name is Polito Padilla. Sure thing, Señora, we will haul the *tierra* away."

"But where is your truck?" I demanded, clinging to what seemed the only stable element in the Padilla situation.

"Oh," grinned this fourth Padilla, "All Santa Fe has to be dug out of mud and muck. We'll get here at six tonight after we've worked all day."

I didn't expect to see even one of the assorted Padilla tribe. But exactly at six, in rolled a huge truck from which jumped four Spanish Americans, all big-hatted and brandishing shovels. I recognized the elderly Polito Padilla who had first appeared at my door, also the youthful Polito who spoke English in the vernacular. Two other men whose voices I had heard over the telephone, were shoveling lustily. They, too, had stated that they were Polito Padilla. And by this time I was feeling more than somewhat confused.

With the four of them shoveling like mad, the driveway was soon cleared of small adobe mountains. When the truck was filled, all scrambled on board and they drove away, but returned to refill it. Then they brushed the driveway. "All through," laughed the youngest Padilla.

A middle-aged Padilla approached with a hastily scrawled accounting. I asked if I should make separate checks for each one.

"No, just one check," smiled the middle-aged Padilla. "I own the business."

Before I even opened my checkbook, I said

firmly, "I'd like to get this matter of you Padilla people straightened out. I'm all mixed up."

The leader of the Padillas roared with laughter. "I own the leetle business, like the card say, to make the furniture, mend the roof, do the cement and adobe work, and haul away *tierra*. That Padilla man not so young ees my uncle. That young fellow is my son. *Naturalmente*, we are all Polito Padillas."

"Yes," I agreed doubtfully, "but that *viejo*— old man— must be your grandfather!"

A little frown spread over the smiling face of the owner of the business. "Señora, that *viejo, pobrecito*, ees not a Padilla at all. Hees real name ees Cesar Basques. But he work for me many years. When teléfono ring een shop, he cannot answer like the rest of us, 'Si, thees ees Polito Padilla.' He do not have one leetle minute when he can feel *importante* like the others. He do now!"

The four Polito Padilla men shook my hand and boarded the huge truck to disappear down my pristine driveway.

The Ancient Rite of Shalako

Every year, sometime in November or December, the Indians of Zuñi Pueblo have for centuries been putting on a ceremonial known as Shalako. It includes a house-blessing rite for all new houses built during the year and much ancient pageantry. Anglos in Santa Fe who have witnessed Shalako hold a kind of Indian-knowledge title of aristocracy.

Many years ago I had spent almost a full day in this remote pueblo, but not at the time of Shalako.

I had been deeply impressed by their red-rock houses. Many of them had small inner doorways so that one could walk from house to house for almost the distance of a city block, and never step outside. I liked the soft voices of the people and the tap-tap of the craftsman's hammer as he fashioned his famous turquoise and silver jewelry. I thrilled to the thought that their sacred Thunder Mountain, with its modern airplane beacon flashing on its summit, still contained on its slopes so much of their ancient ways.

Three of us toyed with the idea. "It's almost a five-hundred-mile trip there and back," I warned. "And in the depth of winter! Shalako comes late this year, just a week before Christmas."

We consulted with friends who had made the expedition last year. "It's an endurance contest," one warned, "but worth it. And cold! Take lots of warm clothes and plenty of food. Buy some long woolen stockings and wear two or three coats."

Another said, "The house-blessing ceremony is inside the new houses. Unless you know a Zuñi, all you can do is to look through the windows and you are welcome to do that. But it gets pretty tiring and cold before morning. You'll never have another experience like it."

By early afternoon of the first day of the ceremony, we were rolling through the wooded hills toward Zuñi. It was a cloudy day promising snow at any moment. We might have to spend Christmas with the Zuñis, we decided. By the time we reached the ancient pueblo among the piney hills, it was raining, a gentle springlike rain that stopped and started at intervals. We had prepared for bitter cold, but needed little of our equipment. The whole red-soiled valley was a quagmire. It was hard to get about in the car, and on foot it was almost impossible. Inside of an hour, both of my high rubber overshoes had been sucked off and lost in that deep red mud.

Word reached us after sundown that the Shalako had come down from Thunder Mountain, had crossed the river, and had entered the Shalako House. Through inky darkness, mist, and mud, we found the Shalako House just as the six gigantic figures, eight-to-ten-feet tall, emerged. They wear massive headdresses of upright eagle and turkey feathers spread like a fan. The great mask face has painted staring eyes, horns on the side, and a wooden beak from which come raucous pipings and clackings. A collar of black feathers and piñon twigs circles the neck. Priceless ropes of turquoise hang down over an embroidered vest. From the figure's

waist, which is the height of a man's head, hangs an enormous black hoop skirt covered by a hand-woven, white ceremonial garment. The motive power of the great figure is a Zuñi under the great skirt. He carries the effigy by means of a pole held in a pocket of his belt. The Shalakos move with a curious birdlike step.

There were five new red-rock houses to be blessed, and a Shalako was assigned to bless each home. We followed the nearest great figure to a new home across from us. The mudheads, whimsical clowns, joined the procession.

The Shalako entered the new house that as yet had no wooden floors. Thanks to the rain and mud, there were only a few people and we were allowed to walk right in. The walls were hung with gay shawls, blankets, and piñon greenery. An open fire was on the hearth and near it white-robed chanters sat in a long line. An attendant sprinkled sacred meal down the middle of the room. The Shalako blessed the walls of the room with sacred meal.

Then a chanter sang in a monotone, hour after hour, from memory. The chant is said to be a kind of Zuñi history from the origin of the people to the present time. When this chanter became weary, another seated beside him picked up the exact word and tone and continued for a time until the head chanter dexterously resumed. This one chant took three hours.

After the ceremony, the people are fed from large supplies of stewed mutton and beef with Zuñi bread baked in outdoor ovens. The dancing usually lasts until daybreak. With dawn comes the ceremonial climax, the race of the Shalakos. Hushed tenseness grips the pueblo. When not one Shalako falls, the pueblo people are satisfied that Zuñi is in a fair way to have another year of good crops and good new homes.

Back of all this pageantry is a core of simple faith that probably accounts for the long history of the old pueblo. Clan and property go down through the maternal line, and women take care of material things. The men are more occupied with their religious duties. They have a saying, "May your road be fulfilled." To have his road fulfilled is all that a Zuñi asks, for he has faith that the road is good. People who know the Zuñis say they are always polite. Faces are pleasant and voices are low. They believe that any bitterness or animosity in the heart renders all their elaborate ceremonial useless.

Back in the sixteenth century, this pueblo was thought to be one of the seven cities of Cibola whose fame and richness were on the tongue of every Spaniard in the shadow of Popocatepetl. The ancient words recited by the caciques in the inner rooms of the red-rock houses are the same now as they were then.

But today every Zuñi child speaks English. There are day schools and a high school. Sewing machines whir in the houses, cars and trucks carry the people here and there. Hydrants flow with piped water, there are electric lights and radios. But still they cling to their ancient ceremonies and the blessing of new houses with the rites of Shalako.

Song for a Soldier

A New Mexico artist found herself in New York City one Christmas season following the war years. She had established herself in a second-story room facing a busy street. The small hotel evidently had been contrived from a large old-fashioned residence which had known better days. It had French doors opening out on a tiny balcony overlooking the street.

Just before midnight, she returned from Christmas dinner with friends. The minute she opened the door to her room, the nostalgic scent of piñon greens greeted her. It evidently came from a big box on the table delivered in her absence.

Quickly she changed into comfortable robe and Indian moccasins. Then she lighted the coal grate of the old-style tiled fireplace. As soon as the fire reached the proper redness, she would toss on a few piñon sprigs if the aroma from that great box fulfilled its promise. Then she would think of New Mexico and happier Christmases.

Hastily she tore the wrappings from the large parcel and extracted boxes of *biscochitos*—New Mexico cookies—with just the right amount of anise scattered through their crispness. She pulled out a dozen small net bags filled with piñon nuts. Carefully wrapped in the bottom of the box was a recording of *La Varsoviana* for the phonograph that accompanied her longer wanderings. Between these gifts, every inch of remaining space had been filled with piñon twigs.

The artist flung a few of the twigs on the red coals of the fire. Immediately the room was filled with their distinctive New Mexico fragrance. Following an old custom, she lighted a single candle and placed it in the front window as village people in New Mexico do, as though to lead the Christ Child to their homes.

Soon the steam-heated room became too warm with the additional heat of glowing coal and burning piñon twigs in the fireplace. The artist flung open the French doors to her small balcony. It was then that she noticed a boy in uniform standing at the edge of the sidewalk. He was sniffing the air like some woodland creature in the great forests of her state. One look at the uplifted face under the glare of street lights convinced the artist that the wan-looking, drooping lad was from some Spanish village not far from her own New Mexico home.

Hardly knowing why she did it, she moved her small record player over in front of the open doors of her balcony. Then she played *Noche de Paz*, the Spanish version of *Silent Night*. From the sidewalk came the shouted request, "*Una vez mas, por favor.*" Over and over that record was played. "Once more, please!"

Was that boy thinking, the artist wondered, as she was, of snow-filled dirt roads leading to adobe villages pocketed in great mountains? Was he thinking of red-flamed piñon pyres burning in the village plaza? Was he thinking of friends and neighbors there, and of the dancing and the lilt of violin and guitar? Perhaps he was thinking of some dark-eyed girl with a gentle voice with whom he had danced in happier days. Whatever it was, the soldier on the sidewalk positively drooped.

A call to the office brought a sleepy desk clerk to her door. "There's a wan-looking little soldier down there on the sidewalk," she explained. "I think, from his appearance, he is from some mountain village in northern New Mexico. Give him these cookies and these bags of piñon nuts. Tell him a lady from New Mexico sends them with Christmas greetings. And—and ask him what village he is from."

From her balcony she watched the transfer of packages to the deep pockets of an army overcoat. Then the telephone rang. "That boy says he is from some village in New Mexico that I just can't get my tongue around, but he says it means trout—you know the fish!"

"Truchas!" the artist exclaimed. "That is the Spanish name for trout. I've been there dozens of times. A beautiful old village which looks as if it were taking off into blue space from the brim of the valley."

The artist went to her balcony again. She put

her new recording of *La Varsoviana* on the little player. She would play it as loudly as she could. That schottische melody had been brought from Warsaw, as its name indicates, by Napoleon's soldiers—at least so the legend insists. It had passed from France into Spain and then to Old and New Mexico. There it became a state of mind. One hears it at grand fiestas in Santa Fe, one hears it back in mountain villages and out on mesalands where shepherds watch their flocks under the glory of the stars.

There were no plaintive pleadings for "once more" from this recording. After several playings of the record, the artist went out on her small balcony to see if her soldier had left. He was standing there straight of back and apparently inches taller. In the direction from which the music had come, he lifted his right arm in farewell. Then he stepped freely on down the sidewalk. His steps still kept the rhythm of the old song. His shoulders rippled with it and his elbows moved like wings against his GI overcoat.

The Wilderness at Hand

I am quite certain that the tall orchard of my neighbor across the lilac hedge is starred as an excellent stopping place for all migrating birds. Fortunately, the windows of my writing room look out on that orchard. I can watch birds by the hundreds flying in on weary wings, squadron by squadron under their top sergeants, until they cover the trees. Here they find water, food, and shelter. That immense tome, Bailey's *Birds of New Mexico*, on my table is as badly worn as the dictionary.

Just a few weeks ago, the most prolific crop of piñon nuts the region had produced in the memory of old residents was picked and carried away by humans, birds, and ever hoarding pack rats. But one unusually tall piñon tree on the top of Chamisa Road kept its nuts still hidden in jewel-box cones. Then suddenly it dropped its enormous crop on the ground. Piñon jays, those large birds of raucous voice and sky-blue plumage, simply preempted the harvest. They so filled the tall evergreen tree that not one green vestige of branch or twig could be seen.

It became a marvel of a tree, a sky-blue tree against the autumn blue of arching sky. Piñon jays in the tree waited in the branches while others on the ground filled their crops. Then others had their turns. There were literally hundreds of them, on the ground, on the tree, and in the air.

But birds are not the only wild creatures which came to New Mexico's capital with its population of some forty thousand at that time. Only a few years ago, following a prolonged drought, bears invaded Santa Fe. Householders could hear garbage cans being overturned by bruins. Bears became so at home in the yards and gardens of Santa Fe that the owners often came across a bear on his hind legs raiding a peach or pear tree, the juice from the stolen tidbit still decorating the raider's jowls.

Deer and that white-splotched, high-jumping creature, the antelope, may be seen from time to time, not many miles from town. Mees Emily and I were only a few miles out on our way to Cerrillos on a dirt road. Suddenly a herd of antelope arched their slight bodies in full flight not a hundred yards from us. So sudden was their appearance and so graceful their flight that they did not seem like living animals, but rather like a superb bas-relief carved by a master craftsman against the ruddy hillside.

Only a short time ago, a half-grown deer invaded Santa Fe, a little over a block from the state's seat of government. The owner of a house-furnishing store looked up one day to see two big ears appearing and disappearing amid couches, chairs, bookcases, and tables filled with dishes and glasses. Thinking that he must be imagining an impossibility, he investigated and gave chase to a half-grown fawn. The chase ended when the frightened visitor jumped into the back of an open display window. Came a crashing of glass, but at long last the pursuer managed to grasp and hold the intruder.

Riot calls were placed with the Game and Fish Department to come at once and help with the struggling dilemma. Two men came on the run and diagnosed the dilemma as a half-grown fawn that had become separated from its mother and had headed down the nearly dry bed of the Santa Fe River nearby. Probably becoming confused by traffic, it had strayed into the comparative quiet of the furniture shop.

The two officials took the adventuring deer in their car back to the forest area from which it had ventured. They said the fawn was big enough to look out for itself even if it did not find its family.

The Little Adobe House on the outskirts of Santa Fe has proved an excellent substitute for the little cabin in the wilderness about which I dreamed long years ago. When that estimable feline, El Hijo de Koshare, who patrols my premises during the early night hours, jumps on my windowsill and scratches to come in, from my couch under the long window, I open it sleepily. I wonder what he has seen outside that makes his fur stand on end and his eyes glitter twice their normal size.

At last he settles down in my cushioned writing chair, for whose possession we dispute by day. "Oh, probably," I say to myself sleepily, "it was only a prehistoric baby *Felis leo*, a remote relative, cavorting around along the leafless lilac hedge."

Cousin Canuto Reverts

Christmas was over, and Cousin Canuto stalked stiffly into the Little Adobe House to tell me about the way they had kept *La Natividad*. "María Lupita and I and Mrs. Apodaca and papá decided to go back to our good old Spanish way of keeping Christmas. We would have no tree with dingle-dangles, no costly presents to pay for later.

"We tell our big boys in newspaper business and they say, 'OK.' We tell our little boys there will be no toys in stockings. On Twelfth Night they can put shoes on the doorstep and the Three Wise Men on camelback will put sweets in their shoes. Little boys cry and say they do not want little old candy in shoes. They want airplanes that fly when they wind them up and long train that runs on little track.

"Mrs. Apodaca tell her family, and Carmencita say, 'Fine, I go to three dances Christmas week. I spend money for new dress and slippers, not for presents for all those *primos*—cousins!' "

Cousin Canuto sighed and helped himself to piñon nuts. "*Los muchachos* and I make enough paper-bag lanterns—*los farolitos*— to put all along the roof of our house. We make two *luminarias* of piled up cedar wood to shine in front of the house. You remember what happened Christmas Eve?"

"It rained," I groaned. With friends I had driven up and down the narrow old streets to see all the houses outlined against the wintry sky with parchment-yellow paper-bag lanterns. But the rain put out the candles and the paper-bag lanterns had become a sodden, collapsed mess.

"Christmas Day was even worse," said Cousin Canuto. "Young Mr. Abeyta come with Apodacas. He know nothing about our plans for a Spanish

Christmas. He bring Mrs. Apodaca two big electric saucepans, and Carmencita a hair-curling iron heated by electricity.

"After a good dinner our boys in newspaper business say they have to go down town, and the Apodacas and Young Mr. Abeyta who shared our dinner say why not go to Casita Apodaca and make some hot chocolate in the new saucepans. Carmencita say the new electric curling iron maybe make her hair look better. But we no more get comfortable in the Apodaca parlor when comes terrible pop-popping out in front and there are our big boys each on a new scooter bike.

"They yell, 'Surprise, surprise! We bought our own presents—twenty-five dollars down on each one and the rest ten dollars a month. Our boss in newspaper business sign papers so we could get them. Listen to the noise we can make!' We listened and it did not sound like *Noche de Paz!* I try hard to have my family know and love old Spanish way of Christmas, and here we were on Christmas Day just buried in electric saucepans, hair curlers and scooter bikes."

"You can't force tradition," I told him between gusts of laughter. I am an Anglo of the Anglos and I had kept a far more Spanish Christmas than he. We had driven up to a mountain village to see modern young Spanish Americans from the high school in Española give the ancient Spanish folk drama of *Los Pastores*—The Shepherds—brought into this country by the earliest Spanish colonists. Some say in 1598.

They gave it in a plain little community house across from an ancient log barn spilling golden hay from an open loft. Horses rambled around at will under the pine trees, and a little burro tagged behind. The young actors played their parts to a packed audience of Spanish Americans—grandparents, parents, and children. There were few Anglos there.

"Ay" nodded Cousin Canuto, "I remember seeing that ancient drama when I was a young boy out in the village of Galisteo. There were few written copies of that ancient play. Words were passed down from father to son and mother to daughter, like a golden ring or a high-backed comb. Memory was the strong chest in which they kept their treasure."

I described to Cousin Canuto how the drama was played all over the front of the room, not on a stage. Over in one corner was a rough little crib and a village girl wrapped in a sky-colored shawl leaning over it. The young actors were dressed in simple garments made in the school. They spoke their lines with sincerity and deep feeling.

"Ay, yes, I remember," sighed Cousin Canuto, *"Los Pastores* are on the way to find and honor the Child. But Lucifer tries to persuade them not to go."

I took up the tale again. The lazy shepherd, Bartolo, wants to sleep all the time, and the little shepherdess, Gila, scolds as she cooks their food over a little fire. The shepherds quarrel among themselves. But St. Michael appears and fights Lucifer. Swords clash and the audience cheers and gasps. But at last, Michael's flashing sword puts a stop to Lucifer's beguilements. The shepherds move on singing toward Bethlehem.

"It all comes back," nodded Cousin Canuto. "Good triumphs over evil once again. That was what that ancient play was all about. Ah, Señora, I want my boys and María Lupita and the Apodacas to see *Los Pastores* next Christmas."

"Do try to see it and take the boys," I urged. "Then it won't matter if the young people have modern ways for Christmas. They have a heritage that neither time nor Anglo inventions can take from them."

Of Gas Meters and Mountains

One of the most beguiling facets of living in Santa Fe is that one encounters drama and poetry amid the most mundane of human activities. This happened to a friend of mine who had established a new home on a hilltop.

She was watering her petunias on the hilltop with its far-flung view of surrounding mountains, when she thought she detected a faint odor of gas coming from the nearby gas meter. A prolonged and closer sniffing of the atmosphere indicated that there was a slight trace of gas mingled with petunia fragrance.

It was out in the open, she thought, and should be harmless. On second thought, she decided to call the company, as a slight leak might indicate something wrong within the house.

The company was most cooperative and agreed to send a man out the next day to investigate. The next morning two men appeared among the petunias. They sniffed and compared sniffs. There was a slight odor of escaping gas.

"Can you fix it?" demanded the owner.

"Tomorrow," smiled the man from the company, "we'll send someone out."

The next day, not one man but three appeared. Two were evidently experts to get the job properly started, and the third a man to do the work. They sniffed and resniffed the atmosphere among the petunias. The consensus was that there was decidedly quite an odor of gas. The workman went inside the house and turned off the gas connection to the range, the water heater, and two furnaces in the basement. Then, under the supervision of the experts, the workman took the gas meter apart. There was a small leak in it which was quickly repaired.

All gas-equipped appliances in the house were turned on again. The two experts and the workman departed with the assurance of men whose work is well done.

But the next morning when the house owner was watering her petunias, the odor of escaping gas was much more evident than it had been before. The company was called again, but could send no one until the following morning.

Then two other men appeared, evidently two more experts, and the same Spanish American workman. All household gas appliances were turned off again. The gas meter, under the direction of the new experts, was again taken to pieces and the new workman instructed what to do about the difficulty. Whereupon, the experts departed for greater problems in the gas profession.

"My name, lady," introduced the workman politely, "is Ambrosio. You have a fine view from your hilltop. Mountains all around!"

"Thank you," acknowledged the owner uneasily. "But what about the leak in the gas meter?"

The middle-aged workman in oil-daubed overalls, faded shirt, and broken-visored cap laughed. "Not a thing I can't fix. It's good to talk with a lady who thinks enough of mountains to build her house where she can see them all around. Even if the soil on this hilltop is full of *caliche*—lime."

He leaned against the warm wall. "My heart is in the mountains," he announced. "I was born in Taos and went to school there. I speak good English. I wanted to stay in Taos because the mountains are closer there.

"It was a good life in Taos. I did a lot of singing there. I have a pretty good voice. I used to sing in the church of my family—mostly in Latin. Then one night I heard the Baptists singing in their church. They sang fine. So I learned their hymns and sang in their church for a couple of years. Then I heard the Presbyterians singing in their church. They sang fine. So I learned their hymns and sang in their choir for three years. They tell me they have a lot of churches in Santa Fe. I want to sing with the Methodists and the Mormons, too. They say they have fine big choirs."

"Why did you come to Santa Fe?" puzzled the owner of the petunias.

"Because I couldn't get enough steady work in Taos to support my family. I had only begun to feel at home here when the company transferred me to a town in the southern part of the state. Not

a mountain in sight! Just endless plains! But now I'm back in Santa Fe with mountains all around. My heart is in the mountains.

"Now take my boy, Ambrosio, Jr. I get him a job with the company. But they send him down south where there isn't a mountain in sight. I tell the company 'That boy's heart is in the mountains. I suffer with him. He has been down on those plains for over a year, eating out his heart for sight of a mountain.'"

"But my gas meter," urged the house owner. "Two men from the gas company came one day, then three the next, and now you and the expert who left. Seven men in all!"

"Oh," explained Ambrosio, "they were mostly experts and couldn't stop a leak if the town was blowing up." He sang a few stanzas from a Baptist hymn and then turned his attention to the petunias. "Your petunias don't look too good. Lots of *caliche* on this hilltop. Fill up the back of the car with paper cartons and go up in the mountains and fill the cartons with good black dirt. Poor little petunias! Their hearts must be in the mountains."

"Did that hymn-singing workman ever get your gas leak repaired?" I asked.

"In no time," laughed the house owner. "To the rhythm of a few verses from *How Firm a Foundation!*"

Light To Sing

Cousin Canuto, with a folded Spanish-language newspaper under his arm, caught me one morning in early summer surveying the ravages of a long, snow-filled winter. The outside adobe plaster would need attention. The turquoise-painted window frames would have to be repainted. The garage roof leaked. The yard was filled with leaves and twigs blown from the silver maple trees which an early snow had covered before they could be raked and burned. I was not feeling particularly happy in spite of flowering fruit trees and amethyst-beaded lilac hedge.

Cousin Canuto seated himself on a wooden box under the white-blossoming plum tree, looking at his Spanish newspaper. "Lots of talk about no jobs for many people," he remarked. "Señora, do you remember the no-job years after the first World War?"

"Do I remember them!" I exclaimed. I had been in the thick of them as a social worker in a great city in California. I had dozens of young, inexperienced workers to direct. We met everything together, from bureaucratic fumbling to local oratory and from riots to glittering threads of comedy.

"I hope you were the kind of social worker who came to the little Spanish village of Los Piñones," Cousin Canuto said. "Sit down on the wheelbarrow and I'll tell you the answer my Tía Altagracia gave to a social worker who called there when I happened to be visiting. That answer has helped me over many a rough spot along the way.

"That village of my Tía Altagracia is on the brim of a deep, rusty-pink arroyo where a little stream runs when rain is plentiful. Even in good years, the people there have little money. Most of them are what you Anglos call subsistence farmers. Usually one man out of every family had to leave home for the summer months to work in the beet fields of Colorado or along the railroad tracks to earn a little cash.

"When the no-job years came, work stopped and, at the same time, the ranchitos produced very little because of little rain. Every family was in a pretty bad way when the social worker appeared in her old Fordcito bumping along the dusty road into the pink arroyo and up the other side to all the little adobe houses.

"I was visiting my Tía Altagracia when the social worker came. It seemed her boss in Santa Fe had told her that she must find out just what each family bought with the money that was given to them. One man she questioned had told her that he had bought his *esposa* a string of *perlas* and another said he had bought a new *automóvil*. The social worker was on the point of tears."

Cousin Canuto refreshed himself with a handful of piñon nuts and moved his box where he could watch a couple of house finches building a new nest in my neighbor's flowering cherry tree.

"In those days, the people of my Tía Altagracia's village seldom saw anyone from outside. They never went anywhere but to Santa Fe by farm wagon to buy lard and beans and flour when their welfare check came. There was no electric wire in her village, no teléfono, no rahdios, not even one run by a battery. When night closed down from the high, cold mountains, there was nowhere to go, no one new to see. It was pretty terrible, Señora—especially in winter.

"At last the social worker managed to tell my Tía Altagracia that she must see what her family had bought with their welfare checks all through the long winter months. My Tía Altagracia brought out the sales slips from the store in Santa Fe. The social worker went over them carefully, one by one, and I noticed she marked one item on each list. She was much more unhappy-looking than my Tía Altagracia.

" 'I just don't see how you feed all this big family on the groceries you can buy with your welfare check,' the welfare lady groaned. 'But why in the world do you buy so much kerosene? You have plenty of piñon for your stove—and I—I don't imagine you sit up and read late at night!' "

"Señora, not one family in the village could

read English in those days and most of them had not seen a Spanish-language newspaper for months. When someone in Santa Fe did give them an old newspaper in Spanish, it was months old, but it went from hand to hand through the village so long that it was in ribbons."

Suddenly I looked at my Little Adobe House and my big adobe lot and decided that they were in surprisingly good condition. They looked positively gilded with peace and plenty.

"I explained to the welfare lady," continued Cousin Canuto, "that my Tía Altagracia built a fire in her stove on winter nights and lighted two big kerosene lamps—one on either side of her room. Nearly all the village came to that room. They brought their babies and my Tía Altagracia put them in rows on her two big beds. Then they sang. At first they sang the songs everyone knew. Then the old ones came with old, old songs written in faded ink on ragged pieces of paper. Some of those songs had come down from the earliest days of Spanish colonization. But the old ones knew them and they taught the others. Everyone sang for hours and they left comforted and happy.

"I told the welfare lady that my Tía Altagracia

became frightened about spending so much of her welfare check for kerosene. So they tried to sing in the dark with only the glow from the piñon fire, but it was no good. They just couldn't sing well in the dark. When I say that, Señora, I look at the welfare lady and she have tears on her face.

"So my Tía Altagracia see the welfare lady to the door and try to explain in her little English. She say, 'We sing a lot here.' Then with gentle eyes but with a firm, strong voice she say, 'You have to have light to sing by.'"

Christmas along an Old Trail

Great-Grandmother Patrocina Padilla insisted that she must see the Christmas lights along the old Santa Fe Trail. All she had ever seen were tantalizing glimmerings and glowings from her thick-walled adobe home under the cottonwood trees, a good two miles from the then little town of Raton in northeastern New Mexico.

For many years, Raton, a town at that time of less than eight thousand people, cradled at 6,600 feet along the base of the Rockies, had been giving a Christmas spectacle of great beauty and religious significance. Time was, not a hundred years ago, when bewhiskered men and calico-skirted women peered with weary eyes from the shelter of white-covered wagons to glimpse even a candle light or two in the little settlement along the old trail.

Now, speeding diesel engines of the Santa Fe railroad, pulling their long silvery caterpillars of trains, pause briefly in Raton and then speed on their way to and from the Pacific Coast. Passengers on them from mid-December to January 2 must wonder what a great thirty-foot angel is doing floating over a hill like a camel's back right in the center of this western town.

All Raton and thousands of visitors through the years know that it is the town's guardian angel which appears every Christmas over Goat Hill where early settlers once pastured their small animals. Along with the shimmering angel against the wintry sky are some twenty other sets scattered along what was once the trail of America's westward march toward the far Pacific.

Most of the figures in these dramatic sets are over eight feet high and floodlighted. They show the Virgin and St. Joseph traveling toward Bethlehem. They show the inn where they were turned away because there was no room for them. They show shepherds watching their flocks by night and the Three Wise Men on their humpbacked camels, lighted by a six-foot star. They show the Nativity scene, the flight into Egypt, and the youthful Christ in the temple.

These are not garish representations. They originated as the work of a young commercial artist, Woodrow Wilson Ballard, who for many years had a dream in his heart. He wanted to tell the Christmas story in a way that everyone, especially children, could understand. Above all, he wanted to do it without any taint of commercialism. He designed, cut the figures out of plywood, and painted them in soft colors. His wife studied reproductions of the old masters to give him costume and color ideas.

The Lions Club of Raton sponsored the project and helped place the figures in cast-iron uprights along the old trail. The town of Raton provided the electricity for the floodlighting, a job that requires three miles of wiring. And to keep commercialism out of their efforts, there is a recorded provision that this Christmas spectacle shall be without one touch of moneymaking and that all the sets be strictly Biblical in content.

The hills that hold this lovely spectacle of

Christmas are wooded with dwarf piñon and cedar trees at their lower levels and with tall pines at their summits. Their piney fragrance encloses the figures with woodland essence. Off to the east stretch the great plains, punctuated by flat-topped mesas and sheer moon-washed cliffs strangely sculptured by sand and storm.

As visitors pass from set to floodlighted set and peer into the darkness between, they must think of other wanderers who passed this way in days gone by. Here stalked Indians through dim mountain passes to the great plains in search of buffalo. Here through these same passes came the first pathfinders feeling their way into the unknown Southwest. Here came Kit Carson, Lucien Maxwell, Céran St. Vrain, trappers, scouts, cattlemen, covered-wagon settlers, and at last the military of the United States. Although unseen, the memory of them is an added luster to this Christmas spectacle which is as timeless as the stars in the wintry sky.

No wonder Great-Grandmother Patrocina Padilla insisted that she must see the Christmas lights along the old trail. Said her sons, "Madrecita, you have too many years and too many pounds. Perhaps we could get you into the Fordcito, but never, never could we get you out."

Said her four stalwart grandsons, "Of a certainty, Abuela—grandmother—must see the lights of Christmas. With two of us on either side, we can get her into the Fordcito and with the help of San Isidro we can get her out again."

So it was that in the line of long, expensive cars and little, ramshackle ones that passed along the old Santa Fe Trail one Christmas night, came a rattling, halting Fordcito in which sat an old, old Spanish-speaking lady swathed in her best black shawl and completely surrounded by big grandsons.

She exclaimed and lifted small brown hands in wonder at sight of the two great white-clad angels that guarded the little town of Bethlehem. She wept when the innkeeper turned the weary travelers away from his door. She sang in quavering voice before the little white church from whose lighted windows came the lilt of Christmas carols.

It was when they passed before the shepherds keeping watch over the sheep that Abuela demanded to get out of the Fordcito. Here was something that a woman of the people knew and understood. Her husband, her brothers, her father, and his father had been shepherds of sheep in this land. She knew their nightly vigils around a pinpoint of campfire in the midst of immensity. She knew how the stars hung over them like gentle chancel lights and how the winds sang their mighty hallelujahs.

The grandsons got Abuela out of the Fordcito by main force and the help of all the saints. They stood at a little distance while she tottered toward sheep and shepherds. Someway, she got to her old, old knees and said her Christmas prayers along the old, old trail.

Carmencita Has Her Song

Pushing back her shawl to indicate that an unhurried visit was in order, Mrs. Apodaca seated herself in the big rocker. "That Carmencita" settled herself on the couch where wide-flung windows opened on the summer night. The scent of honeysuckle floated in and the soft whispering of leaves stirring along the lilac hedge and on the silver maples. Great stars blazed like campfires along the blue trailways overhead.

Carmencita had brought her arithmetic to study while her mother and I talked. A future recruit for the U Esse Air Force of the middle 1960's could not waste her time while her mother and I talked. She was "square-rooting," she explained.

"We were a leetle worried," confessed Mrs. Apodaca, "that when you went away to that town called Raton way up near Colorado that you might like it better than Santa Fe. You should know, Señora, that the Spanish word, *ratón*, means mouse. How would you like to live in a town whose name means mouse? You who love words that sing!"

"That small town sings," I protested, "whatever its name may mean. It sings with the roll of wagon wheels of western-bound America. Even after almost a hundred years, I heard the song of the old Santa Fe Trail there. It was the song of hundreds of white-covered wagons crawling foot by foot over the Pass of the Mouse to drop down into the lovely valley which now holds the town of Raton. It has wooded mountains on one side and a backdrop of mesa tops and towering buttes on the other."

Mrs. Apodaca shuddered. "Señora, I deed not know you went there on horseback."

"I didn't," I laughed. "Now a fine hard-surfaced road leads out of the town and up over the

131

Pass of the Mouse. Cars skim over it as effortlessly as cumulous clouds along the skyways."

Reassured on this point, Mrs. Apodaca leaned back in the old rocker. "What was the song you heard, Señora?"

I said that I heard the song of heavy wagon wheels as they climbed foot by foot over this last terrible barrier that stood in the way and the equally heartbreaking descent with roped wheels into the hollow where the town now stands. Axles cracked, wheels splintered on rocks, animals groaned and fell to the ground. Heavy cargoes had to be lightened and cherished pieces of furniture were left beside that vertically spiraling trail.

Following the covered wagons came the lighter notes of stagecoaches bumping into the old town. After that came the hoofbeats of the pony express playing its staccato music through the night as Lincoln's latest message was carried to towns springing up along the western sea. Forts sprang up across the desert. Shrill and clear came the sound of bugles in the high, dry air as the cavalry galloped out to put down an Indian uprising, to rescue an emigrant train, or to protect a tiny settlement. "I heard all this song in the Town of the Mouse," I said.

Carmencita kept right on square-rooting.

"Ah," exclaimed her mother, "that was a fine song you heard, Señora. But there are older songs than that in our region, hundreds of years older, made by my people. Those songs are not made by wagon wheels. They are made by the hoofbeats of horses and mules, and flocks of sheep and goats, and herds of cattle crawling along slowly over the desert, past dry waterholes with *los Indios* hiding behind the beeg rocks. For a long time we poor people had no wagons at all—only leetle wooden carts weeth beeg solid wheels made of wood. There was one good theeng about those carts. For a long time before they came in sight, my people could hear the terrible squeaking of those solid wood wheels on wooden axles. That gave them time to heat up *los frijoles* and to pat out more tortillas for the newcomers. I, too, Señora, have heard about the song of the trail of my people."

And the Indians, too, must have a song of the trail, I mused. Before the Spanish came in, the Indians were neither on horseback nor did they have the wagons my people brought in. They walked. They padded far down into Mexico to the court of Montezuma to trade the sky-blue turquoise for parrot feathers and shells from a tropical, palm-shaded shore. They padded out to the great plains to hunt

133

the buffalo. Out near Puyé, I have had my own feet in trails theirs have worn in the solid rock by centuries of ceaseless padding back and forth.

We sat quietly thinking of the old trails of our region and the color and high romance that flowed along them. We heard the whisper of the song that flowed along the Indians' Turquoise Trail, and the beat of hoofs and the wild uproar of covered wagons along the Santa Fe Trail. The song of these trails blended into one melody and sang in our hearts.

"That Carmencita" kept right on square-rooting. With long black braids hanging neatly beside an intent little face, with highly polished near-military shoes placed firmly on the floor, with lean shoulders held as erect as if even now they wore a uniform, Carmencita kept her mind on the extraction of square roots.

"Ay," grieved her mother, " the poor *muchachos!* The trails have all reached the Pacifico and can go no further. *Muchachas* like Carmencita will hear no songs of the trails."

Suddenly a light appeared in the segment of dark sky outside the far-flung window. It flashed through the summer night like an elongated star. With the flashing came the drone of powerful motors.

134

Carmencita dropped her square roots to the floor as she jumped to her feet and stood peering out with enraptured attention at the vast arc of summer sky. "Sounds like a big Connie," she exclaimed with a lilt in her voice as the great Constellation swept by. "New York, London, India, Japan, San Francisco—and Space and Space and Space!"

Song of a Little House

The Little Adobe House in Santa Fe is singing its Christmas song. Long before and after the day, the song is high and clear with an undertone of contented humming that lingers through the calendar of days.

This is the setting of the song. Picture the narrow, crooked streets of the old town, its snow-topped, high adobe walls, its clusters of flat-roofed, cubical, little houses like children's blocks scattered over the wintry landscape.

Around about, like the sides of a yellow mixing bowl, are golden hills where pigmy forests of brown-coned piñon and lavender-berried juniper grow as if planted by elfin gardeners. Beyond the hills to the east and north are great mountains, peacock blue in the clear winter light. Their summits are so heaped with snow that they seem ethereal, floating in a sea of ever changing radiance.

A little frozen river almost cuts the town in two. Off to the south and west are buttes and straight-edged mesas, like solidified spectra, rose, yellow, and indigo. Overhead at night, big stars move so close at hand one can almost hear the melody of their ordered passage. Down in the southern hills twinkles the campfire of some solitary shepherd, watching his flocks by night. Up toward the mountains blossom little piñon fires along many a thread of lonely road leading to snow-imprisoned adobe villages.

Unhurriedly, up and down the streets of Santa Fe walk people of three cultures, taking in the sights of Christmas. Indian women in knee-high, white doeskin boots peer delightedly from under heavy, gay-colored shawls at Wise Men and camels atop the flat-roofed hotel. Long-skirted, black-shawled, Spanish-speaking women lead their *muchachos* to see a manger scene in a lighted window. Cowboys in high-peaked hats and bright shirts mince ludicrously along in high-heeled boots.

The Little Adobe House has its own decorations. Paper bags, half-filled with sand in which burn lighted candles, outline in parchment yellow the lovely lines of its flat roof. Others mark the turquoise-blue gate to a small patio.

When you step inside, you will think for a moment that you are in the midst of a forest far remote from the world. The low ceiling is a mass of piñon boughs as if the cinnamon-colored ceiling beams had sprouted green fragrant branches. From ceiling to floor every corner is banked with juniper and cedar. Every picture and window frame is outlined with feathery blue-green spruce—the same spruce the Indians use to usher the year on its way.

In the white corner fireplace burn piñon logs, stood on end like an indoor campfire. Their resinous flame paints the white walls pink and decorates them with dancing shadows of greenery and candlelight. In the blue-painted *nicho*, choristers in the form of candles sing in a miniature forest of long-needled pine. Geraniums, crimson, rose, and white, bloom in a deep windowsill. Candles in tin holders make little pools of light in the shadowy room.

Koshare, the cat who started life in Tenorio Flat, sits on the Navajo saddle blanket before the fire and adjusts the enormous ruff of his winter furs. But he keeps wise eyes on the deep canopy of greenery overhead. "Who knows," thinks Koshare, "a bluebird might easily pop out of those branches and tweak my plume of a tail in an excess of holiday exuberance."

Faces appear outside the deep-set window. Noses are flattened against the panes as big eyes stare at fire and candlelight. On the outskirts of Santa Fe, it is expected that people will look in at Christmas windows. Mrs. Apodaca and her friends even arrange holiday windows for all to see with a manger scene and lighted candles and their best geraniums.

Some of the window-gazers venture into the house. As naturally as a flight of birds, they come to rest before the fireplace. There they burst into song —old Spanish carols learned at home and English carols learned at school. I keep wishing for an Indian chanter and the beat of a *tombé* to make our three-peoples Christmas complete and symbolic of the Peace on Earth promised by angel voices over golden hills much like our own.

When the last singer has left, crunching through the snow toward Tenorio Flat, I sit by the ruddy embers and wonder what is the charm of this forest-green, forest-fragrant, simple, little house. Perhaps it is that, once a year at Christmas time, the beauty of forests, elfin trees, print of deer tracks in the snow, and boundless skies move into the Little Adobe House.

After all, so much of the lovely Christmas story took place out of doors. There was the long donkey-back journey to Bethlehem. There were shepherds going about their everyday tasks who saw a star and heard the song of angels under dark skies. There was a manger to which the mild-eyed beasts of the field, as well as the hosts of Heaven, had access.

This is the theme of the song of the little house that rises high and clear at Christmastime and lingers in a contented humming through the calendar of the days.

Blue Spruce Christmas

For all the joys of Christmas confined in the Little Adobe House, the reality is found far afield. Upward-blowing flame wings in the corner fireplace, shadows of candlelight on thick white walls, fragrance of piñon boughs and blue-berried juniper, are but samples of a larger beauty.

Every year the topmost peak of Christmas joy is experienced out of doors. Going after Christmas greens is the excuse offered for wanderings that may take us only to piñon forests not far from Tenorio

Flat or a hundred miles away. There have been piñon Christmases and silver fir and mistletoe Christmases. Each year the wintry wanderings have been different and the predominating greenery in the little house tells the story of where I have been. Of all of them, the blue spruce Christmas lingers as the most highlighted in my memory.

Perhaps the charm of blue spruce in my memory is emphasized by its connection with pueblo-dwelling Indians. Seldom a ceremonial dance was given in the old days that the dancers' elbows and ankles were not twined with tufts of blue spruce. The women dancers carried tufts of it in their hands and waved it stiffly in precise gestures to the right and to the left, in time with the drums and the fervent voices of the chanters.

Several carloads of us started out one week before Christmas for the Jemez Mountains in whose shadow doze some of the most colorful and least touched Indian pueblos. It was one of those turquoise-blue days that New Mexico produces in early winter. The atmosphere was so saturated with blue, it seemed that a white handkerchief waved from a window must be colored instantly as if dipped in dye.

As soon as we crossed the Rio Grande, we were

in a perfect spider web of dirt roads, unmarked and bewildering. Although we had no intention of visiting an Indian pueblo, we found ourselves in Cochiti. All the little square houses were golden in the sunlight. Husked corn in all the colors of the rainbow, was stacked like wood on top of flat roofs. It was a luminous village where bright-shawled women and men with gay silk bands about their heads went about their concerns of flocks and fields. Always, spruce greens in the little adobe house will include a golden Indian pueblo under a turquoise sky.

Finally by dint of much climbing, we reached the high, dim, mountain pockets where the spruce forests lift their silver crowns. Immediately the party separated to do their own individual gleaming. Up here the air was rarer and colder. Vestiges of an early snow lay like scrollwork between the leafless bushes and dried ferns. A fragrance of moist, rich soil, dried leaves, and sun on evergreen branches filled the air. As I searched up and down the slopes, I had trouble to keep my mind on the perfect little silver-blue tree that was the object of my search.

A coyote stood on top of a rocky precipice and eyed my intrusion of his domain with some amazement. A flock of wild pigeons, like miniature airplanes, zoomed across a ravine. The ever present, blue-winged piñon jay shouted insulting imprecations.

At last, I found the perfect little tree with its blue-green needles showing a silvery bloom. But alas, all the hatchets were with the men of the party now cutting down bigger trees at a higher level. All I had was a pair of clippers and they were very dull. But imitating the beaver, I chewed with those dull clippers around and around the trunk until, by sheer persistence, I could swing the little tree to my shoulder and bear it in triumph to the car.

It was night before we got down to the Rio Grande on our return. We must have looked like animated forests along the dark road. Back in the shadow-filled hills was Cochiti. The windows of Santa Ana pueblo showed orange lamplight across the river. A star hung over the black mesa of Zia. A shepherd had built a little fire between sheltering hills where his flock was sheltered for the night.

Not just branches of blue spruce moved into the Little Adobe House that night. The memory of Jemez Mountain moved into the little house in all its snow-capped splendor. So did the dark whisper of the Rio Grande which had seen so many, many men come and go through the centuries. So did the star hanging over skyey Zia on its mesa top.

Etiquette in a Blizzard

One night during the last part of January, when snow and ice made the approaches to the Little Adobe House decidedly hazardous, I found Mrs. Apodaca and Carmencita rapping on my door. Mrs. Apodaca, wrapped in several layers of shawls like a cocoon, extinguished the old kerosene-burning tin lantern she was carrying in spite of Carmencita's modern flashlight. They had brought newspapers on which to place their mud-caked boots. Whenever she had a chance, Carmencita winked at me. Mamacita was evidently displeased about something. After polite conversation, it dawned on me that I was the object of that displeasure.

At last, Mrs. Apodaca removed a Chimayo blanket, the outmost layer of her cocoon, and looking sadly at me asked, "Señora, excuse it please, but why you ride all over town een the beeg *troque* of Agapito Blea just after that terrible snow? Right up on the beeg front seat weeth Agapito on one side of you and hees helper, Filadelfo Cassados, on the other!"

Trying to keep laughter out of my voice, I explained that I just had to get my mail. I have a post office box downtown and so does the violinist in my front house. The violinist works downtown and usually brings my mail to me every day. But there were many days during that great snow when she could not get her car out and drive downtown. As days passed, we knew that our boxes would be packed solid with accumulated papers and magazines and, worst of all, with letters which might need attention. Having our mail became an obsession with us.

Mrs. Apodaca shrugged shawl-draped shoulders at such foolishness as I explained further that

I also needed many things from Benito's market. There was very little food left in my house.

"Benito have leetle *troque*," argued Mrs. Apodaca. "Why not call heem on teléfono and he would breeng theengs to you?"

I protested that Benito's light truck could not possibly get through the snow drifts and mud on San Antonio Street. Neither could the violinist's car get out so that she could extricate our mail from overflowing boxes in the post office downtown.

"So you use teléfono and ask Agapito to drive you een hees beeg *troque*, all over town!"

"Yes, and I say I will pay him and his helper just as if he were shoveling snow. Agapito not only has a powerful truck, but heavy snow tires on it. He and Filadelfo shoveled a little path so the violinist and I could get to each other's houses and then I climbed into that big truck and rode downtown to the post office where it took me ages to dig out our two crammed boxes."

"And then," prompted Mrs. Apodaca.

"Then we went to Benito's Market. We all went in. No one was in the little store but Benito. He was happy to have someone to talk with about the great snow. I bought a huge box of groceries and then we stood around and talked for awhile.

The big truck brought us home and Agapito carried the big box of groceries into my kitchen." It was a lark—that trip. I wouldn't have missed it for anything. Hardly anyone was out on the streets. It looked like the old Santa Fe I knew when I first came here over twenty years ago.

"But what if you fall on ice or *troque* skid and turn over?"

"It didn't and I didn't," I laughed, and tossed another piñon log on the fire. I would never forget that ride in the big truck beside the frozen river and along the almost deserted streets of our old town which has seen stranger sights than me perched between two Spanish workmen on Agapito's high truck seat.

Mrs. Apodaca was still shaking her head when I brought in yellow cups filled with her favorite hot chocolate and some of Benito's not too inspiring store cookies. Maybe because of the glowing fireplace, maybe because of the hot chocolate, Mrs. Apodaca became her own delightful self. We laughed and talked about our dramatic country. That tremendous fall of snow would put aside all possibility of drought for another summer. Our great forests would be green and beautiful. All our streams and rivers would run bank-deep with water.

Then Mrs. Apodaca sat upright and made her position clear. "Señora, please excuse me and all my talk about you riding around weeth Agapito and Filadelfo een beeg *troque*. That was not what make me unhappy. Was sometheeng else."

"Tell us, Mamacita, tell us," begged Carmencita.

"I weel tale," nodded Mrs. Apodaca. "Een old days when theengs are bad like snows and mucho ice and leetle food een houses, peoples turn to their *amigas* for help. Everyday I look at nize theengs I make to eat and I ask papá to keep leetle path shoveled between our two adobes. I theenk, *mi amiga* who leeves een leetle adobe house, weel come over to borrow some theengs from me. Maybe bread, maybe potatoes! I weel geeve her what she ask and more. I weel geeve her enchiladas and tamales and the leetle fried pies she like so much.

"You do not come, Señora," sighed my neighbor. "Een the old days when theengs are bad, peoples go to their friends. I look and look at all the nize theengs I have to eat een my kitchen. I make more and more. You deed not come, Señora. I am sad. But I deed not know about the deeg out the mail boxes you have to do een U Esse Post Oficina. I never get a letter."

The Wire Electrica

Ay, breathed Mrs. Apodaca, stretching small brown hands toward fireplace glow, "my Indian friend, Prudencia Cheeken, come to see me. She ees grandmamá of the beeg Cheeken family een the Indian pueblo near the veelage where I grow up. Always the Cheeken family and our family are *amigos*. She tale me many unhappy theengs how Indian peoples peek up ways of Anglos."

"But tell me first," I gasped, "how could an Indian woman have the name of Prudencia Chicken?"

"Oh," exclaimed Mrs. Apodaca calmly, "een old days when Indians go to U Esse Indian School, teachers theenk sometimes leetle Indians better have American first name. So they geeve leetle girl name of Prudence wheech we Spanish call Prudencia. Then they ask man teacher who know some Indian talk, what leetle Prudencia's last name mean in Tewa. Man say 'Cheeken' and that ees her name to this day and she ees now grandmamá."

"What unhappy things are the Chicken people doing?" I prompted.

"Indians een that pueblo have now the wire electrica," explained Mrs. Apodaca. "The married son of Prudencia Cheeken have the electrica refreeg, the rahdio, the TV, the wash machine, and the blanket electrica for the bed. They have no gas line and use wood stoves."

The electric blanket for the bed reminded me of a most delightful sight in our plaza during the last cold weather. On one of the metal Spanish-type benches sat an old, old Indian with his long black braids dangling in front of his ears. He was wrapped in an electric blanket from his chin to his feet. That blanket looked like one he had found in some trash can and, of course, there was no place to plug it in, even if it worked, as it probably didn't. But that old

Indian was simply radiating comfortable warmth from his half-closed eyes to his moccasined feet. I told this story to Mrs. Apodaca, who smiled but evidently did not get the picture nor its implications.

"But how does the Chicken family pay for all those expensive electric luxuries?" I questioned.

"The husband of Prudencia Cheeken have good labor job at Los Alamos and so have their son who have wife and four darling cheeldren. But day labor weel not pay for all those nize theengs electrica. They get *dinero* from Happy Day Loan Company.

"Grandpapa Cheeken and hees son put names on paper wheech they never read. But when they do not pay on loan for two months, men from Happy Day Loan Company come out to pueblo and say if they do not pay, they weel take their houses and their lands to pay for all those nize theengs. Cheeken men laugh and laugh because lands do not belong to them. They belong to pueblo.

"After a long, long time Cheeken family get some of their nize, nize theengs paid for. The son of Prudencia go to hees papá and say, 'You and I need big home freeze for our families. You borrow half of money and I borrow half. You keep home freeze in your house half of year, I keep it other half.'

"They get beeg, beeg home freeze and put names to many, many dollars. Then winter come and lots of days weeth no work. So two men from Happy Day Company come to pueblo and say, eef do not pay, they weel take the beeg home freeze away. They say they weel take their other so nize theengs too.

"When Prudencia Cheeken hear all thees sad talk, she say, 'Don't do anything until we go see Mees Emily in Santa Fe.'

"Mees Emily send them home to breeng every piece of paper they ever sign for loan company. Then she make them take back beeg home freeze and the TV set and meexer to the Happy Day people. Then she go to the Happy Day peoples and feex eet so they can keep paying on refreeg and wash machine.

"All ees quiet for long time and then Happy Day Company call Mees Emily and say that both Cheeken men are een oficina and they want loan to buy leetle tractor. They theenk they can rent tractor to other pueblo people for pueblo lands. Mees Emily go right down to oficina and say, 'You know the same as I do that your pueblo elders stay with old ways. You know the same as I do that Earth Mother is used to hand tools and she will not give any harvest if you run tractor over her.' They do not get loan.

"After Mees Emily get eet all feexed, she go out to pueblo and talk weeth governor and then she go home and collapse. I have to go to her house every day for long time to run eet and answer teléfono. Eet ees nice to work een her house. She do not have the deesh-wash electrica, she do not have the meex-er electrica. She do not have wash the clothes electrica.

"But she do have the home freeze electrica. Eet ees the biggest I ever see. Some Anglo lady moving away from Santa Fe geeve eet to Mees Emily. May-be you never see eet. Eet ees so beeg, Mees Emily keep eet on her *portal* weeth leetle wire coming out of window to run eet."

"What in the world can Miss Emily, a woman alone, find to put in that enormous home freezer?" I asked.

Mrs. Apodaca gave me a knowing smile. "I do not know what she keep een eet een weentertime, but I know what she keep een eet een summer."

"What does she keep in it in summer?"

"From April teel November," she smiled, "Mees Emily keep her beeg, long fur coat een that deep freeze. Not one moth!"

Christmas in the Mountains

N o one really knows a little adobe house, Mary Austin says in her *Land of Journey's Ending*, until the adobe roofs are muffled with snow and cedar flames run up the walls of three-cornered chimneys. Many winters, and especially many Christmases, have taught me the deep sense of companionship a snow-shawled little adobe house can give.

But I still maintain that snow, muffling flat roofs, clinging to golden adobe walls, and decorating rainbow-colored mesaland, is sheer fantasy and play-acting. It has the quality of a child tilting along in its mother's high-heeled shoes—swishing about in trailing skirts and eclipsed by an adult's hat resting precariously on its ears. Snow around Santa Fe usually gives the same whimsical effect. Almost you can hear it begging, "Look at me! See what I can do!"

A snowbound Christmas on Cinnamon Mountain, in the midst of an elfin forest of piñons and cedars, showed me the variations possible within a few miles of Santa Fe. Here snow was not a show-off prank, but an austere reality.

Margot and Judy had acquired a little house near Cinnamon Mountain—a house that looked for all the world like a woodchopper's cabin in some old fairy tale. It was built of yellow pine slabs whose rough bark repeated the warm tones of the ruddy mountain upon which it had grown. All around, spread head-high forests of evergreens. To one side, the forest dipped down to desert and distant ruddy mesas. Back of it reclined a row of mountain giants, carved from reddish sandstone. Below the bald pate of timberline, on their rocky craniums, grew a slight fuzz of pine and fir. And all their waistcoat pockets were lined with cedar.

The inside of the cinnamon-stick house was all one room, its walls and ceiling of yellow pine boards. Windows with little square panes looked out on purple buttes and recumbent giants. A big iron cookstove purred like a huge cat and gave off a perpetual aroma of cedar. Margot's big press for the delicate etchings she made stood in one corner. Cots with fuzzy blankets marched down the sides. Books in four languages filled homemade shelves. Kerosene lanterns and a battered guitar hung from the rafters.

Margot and Judy had rescued me from a lonely Christmas in what was then a new way of living. They had taken me out in their ancient car with the fish-wagon posterior, to spend a snowy Christmas in the shadow of Cinnamon Mountain.

We stalked through translucent curtains of snow to pick Christmas greens. Mistletoe grew in clumps as big as basketballs on the ragged red limbs of cedar trees. Oddly enough, New Mexico mistletoe reflects both the desert in its sage-green foliage and the sea in its berries as big as pearls in a necklace and sea-shell pink.

Armed with clippers we were able to bring armload after armload into the cinnamon-stick house. We heaped the corners, we banked the bookshelves, we draped the rafters. By way of contrast, we added cedar boughs dotted with lavender berries showing a silver bloom. The big stove winked more and more furiously and drew out the essence of miles of forestland in that one small room. Still the snow came down and the wind-organ let out all its stops.

About midnight of that snowy Christmas Eve, suddenly there came a great silence. The wind-organs stopped playing. The trees stopped their rappings against cinnamon-stick walls. An utter quiet lapped about us in the fragrant, green room. A soft light sifted through the little square-paned windows. We opened the door to look out on a serene, quiet world stretching in silver waves as far as the eyes could reach. Stars seemed suspended on dazzling filaments in a sky so close that it gathered to itself mesa's edge and mountain summit. Here was not whimsy, but reality.

Across that pristine world of silver and lilac shadows, came the long-drawn wail of an animal in distress. Desolation and terror were in that cry.

"It must be Remedio's little dog," Margot said. "The ranchito is on the other side of the next hill. Remedio and Mamacita and four *muchachos* passed by early this morning in the wood wagon with two old horses pulling it. They were on their way to spend Christmas with relatives near Glorieta. I hope they got there without too much trouble in all this snow. I'm sure they had a dog with them."

"Maybe he slipped out," suggested Judy, "and wandered back home over the hills."

We tried to forget that plaintive wailing of a small dog, but we could not. In the end, booted, sweatered, and blanket-wrapped, a procession of three, carrying kerosene lanterns, struggled through the drifts. Sometimes we were on the trail, sometimes off and clinging to the trunks of cedar trees. At last, on Remedio's sagging *portal*, we found a small, shivering dog. We took turns carrying him under our blankets on the way home.

Warm and reassured by the presence of human folk, the little dog did not so much as move a whisker when we came across two magnificent deer almost at the door of the cinnamon-stick house. With delicate feet they were pawing the snow from Judy's iris plants. Starlight dappled their dun coats. They stood there eying us, unafraid as deer should stand, early on Christmas morning.

Mees Emily's Masquerade

Last winter Mees Emily and I sat by my corner fireplace and talked about spring. "Do you remember your first spring in Santa Fe?" she asked. "I remember mine almost a quarter of a century ago. It was much like many others I was to experience, with frayed and torn nightcaps of snow on the high mountains and the valley of the Rio Grande shouting with bank-to-bank runoff. Blue birds by the dozens were spreading their wings over greening chamisa sage and from the Indian pueblos came the throb and beat of waist-high drums making ready for corn-planting dances.

"A few years ago I was remembering all this as I walked about my patio garden. Everything in it was just as it should be. Irises were blooming purple, blue, white, and yellow along my walks. The wild plum hedge was as white with blossoms as the mountains were with fraying snow. 'Oh,' I thought to myself, 'how I'd like to be a first-time tourist here for a few days.'

"Why not? I was rather at loose ends as my daughter had left for a prolonged stay in California. The more I thought about it, the better it seemed. I would be a turista!"

Ever since I have known Mees Emily, I have never seen her in conventional attire. Years ago on the Navajo Reservation, she had acquired the pattern for the lovely dresses she has since worn—full skirts, bodices cut on straight lines. I've never seen her with a hat or conventional jacket or shoes on her feet. She always wears Indian moccasins. "What did you do about clothes?" I puzzled.

"Raided my daughter's clothes closet," she laughed. "We are pretty much the same size. I found a couple of suits, a dress or two, a jacket, shoes, and even a hat. I had to change my Navajo hairdo

162

for that hat, and I actually didn't know myself when I looked in the mirror.

"I packed a suitcase for a week's trip. Out in the garage I found a discarded box camera and an armful of ancient, highly colored, tourist-bureau folders which some visiting friend had left behind. I also carried a neatly rolled silk umbrella from my conventional days.

"Almost at nightfall, I called a cab and was driven to a small hotel particularly favored by ladies traveling alone. I registered under my maiden name and address and asked how far it might be to the plaza."

Mees Emily and I sat rocking with laughter at this, as she probably knows every street in Santa Fe almost as well as she knows her own walled patio.

"The desk clerk was very helpful," she went on. "He produced a map which he kindly red-penciled with routes, not only to the plaza, but to museums, art galleries, shops, and ancient adobes.

"I slept well in a comfortable bed in a plain little room and breakfasted on superb blueberry pancakes. Three women sat down at my table, and before the meal was over we had agreed to do the town together."

Mees Emily leaned back in the big rocker and

laughed until she wept. "You should have seen us tearing from museum to museum, gallery to gallery, and from gift shop to gift shop. I carried my old camera, my tightly rolled silk umbrella and my armful of tourist-bureau pamphlets. Some of my Santa Fe friends passed quite close to me and never gave me a second glance.

"We took sightseeing trips to nearby Indian pueblos and to Spanish villages. You know I have friends in all those places and I was quite panicky that my disguise be penetrated.

"But fortunately, everyone was busy slapping fresh adobe plaster on little houses, or plowing their fields, or driving out their stock, or cleaning their big beehive ovens. They had no eyes for the turistas who ohed and ahed at sight of their workaday activities.

"The day before my companions were to leave, we took one of Santa Fe's little buses and rolled up Canyon Road. Suddenly we were almost opposite my own home. I pressed the bell for the driver to stop. 'Let's prowl around here on foot,' I suggested. 'It looks interesting.'

"Do you know what I did? I led them into my own patio. They followed me, shaking in their shoes in case they might be caught trespassing. I had never

seen my patio so lovely. The big pear tree had come
into shimmering bloom, the irises were shaking out
masses of silken banners, white pigeons were skim-
ming overhead, and the high adobe wall gave off
a copperish glow in the sunlight. 'Do I actually live
here?' I wondered, Suddenly I wanted to be home.

I rushed my protesting companions back to the hotel, said my farewells, and checked out. Then I taxied as fast as I could urge the driver along the way to my adobe.

"I got out of my ridiculous clothing and into my ample full-skirted dress and my heavenly comfortable sandals. I used the armful of tourist-bureau pamphlets to start a fire in my corner fireplace. I fed the pigeons copiously and picked an armful of irises of all colors and shades to grace my desk. Then I sat in my big, worn, old chair and thought and thought half of the night."

We both sat looking into my open fire, chuckling with it and our own thoughts. At last Mees Emily said quietly, "That first spring which we both experienced long years ago was a song set to dance music, a thing of the eyes, the ears, and the nostrils. But the spring I saw last year was a song of old, old rhythms. The Indians sense this and express it in their beautiful ceremonials, in their crafts, and in their art. So do the Spanish people in Chimayo and the other little villages in their beautiful weaving and even in the way they hang crimson chiles to dry along their adobe house walls. It is a sense of belonging. It is the awareness of deep, strong roots as well as fragile bloom."

Christmas Eve in San Felipe

Beside the Rio Grande, on the west bank, the Indian pueblo of San Felipe spread out before us like an oriental print in the weird greenish light of a lopsided moon.

Along the edge of the pueblo we could see silhouetted against the sky the dim outlines of the two belfries of one of the oldest and most beautiful churches in New Mexico. This was Christmas Eve, and we had come to witness the dances which we had been told were enacted each Christmas before the two-hundred-year-old altar of this Franciscan mission.

We sat in our car drinking cups of hot bouillon from our thermos bottles, and eating sandwiches. In a few of the thick-walled adobe houses a candle flickered in the window, but otherwise there appeared to be no sign of life inside. A few Indians wrapped in blankets passed silently as ghosts through the empty streets. We wondered if, for reasons unknown to us, the midnight mass and the accompanying dance ritual was to be omitted this year.

Then from the distance we heard the muffled beat of Indian drums. We followed the eerie sound through piñon trees leading to the church.

When we pushed open the heavy hand-carved doors, we found ourselves in another world. Thick adobe walls, freshly whitewashed, soared to a dim high ceiling. Down the center of the nave, a wire had been stretched, on which half a dozen lanterns made orange-colored balloons in the dimness. Halfway down the walls on either side, tall iron stoves fairly vibrated with burning cedar wood. Up ahead in the shadows, candles lighted the high altar. Indians and Spanish and Anglo visitors seated themselves on blankets spread on the hard-packed adobe floor or propped themselves along the cold walls. All around surged muted conversations in English, Spanish, and several Indian dialects.

High up under the shadowy roof, in a choir loft in the rear, young Indians practiced choral responses for the midnight mass. A little nun pedaled a melodeon and led the singing. The old choir loft groaned and creaked with each footstep and each crescendo of laboring organ and young voices.

The priest and an Indian boy came to the altar. The padre intoned the service in a rich, mellow voice, and the nun and her charges answered from the choir loft. Immediately the adobe floor was filled with blanket-wrapped, kneeling people. One old Indian near me was so completely shrouded in a great thick blanket and remained so motionless that I wondered if he could possibly be alive. He made no responses. He never changed his position. Enclosed in his teepee-like blanket, he simply disappeared from all contact with the scene into a world of his own.

In the midst of the service, two young Indian couples went forward to the altar rail and were married in a simple ceremony which included the wrapping of a stole about each couple's shoulders. The brides showed no wedding finery, unless bright shawls pulled down to their eyebrows and deerskin boots with twinkling silver buttons were the equivalent. It was a touching, beautiful service, but it was in a minor key.

Almost before the last response of children's voices had faded into shadowy space, came the staccato, hair-raising throb of Indian drums. Indians sprang to their feet. The old fellow beside me came suddenly alive. The center of the church was cleared. People packed themselves along the great thick walls. The scent of spruce boughs, burning cedar chunks, guttering candles, incense, and woolen blankets filled the place. Excitement sped like an electric current from person to person.

In came the drummers, pounding as if ten thousand devils were to be driven from the scene. In whirled dozens and dozens of dancers in the gayest, most exuberant dance I had ever seen in all my years in this land of Indian dancing.

Although these were Pueblo Indians, they were dressed in Navajo finery—the women in layers of full, swaying skirts, rainbow-colored velveteen basques, the men in levis and pink, blue, or purple shirts. Turquoise pellets dangled from their ears, silver chains and coral and turquoise ornaments swayed inch-deep around their necks. Bracelets jangled and flashed on uplifted bronze arms. Rattle gourds beat out a rhythm such as we had never heard. It sounded like pebbles tossed by an exultant sea along an endless shore. Here was no minor key. Here was joy let loose.

It was not the quiet joy of the Christmas service. The Indians returned to an earlier, more primitive joy known when the world was young. It was as penetrating as sunlight, it was as unrestrained as winds blowing over the great plains. It was whirling, ever active color. It was rhythm moving in upsweeps of sound like bird notes in untouched forests. The faces of Indian spectators glowed like cedar fires, Spanish Americans moved their bodies to the insistent tempo, Anglo faces lost their masks of worry and restraint.

I went over to the old Indian who had disappeared deathlike under his blanket during the early part of the ceremony. He was very much alive now. His eyes were shining. His face glowed with emotion. His old body was erect and tense with the rhythm. "What do you call that dance?" I asked, hoping he could speak English. "It is the most beautiful I have ever seen."

"Navajo Dance, Navajo Dance," he chanted, hardly taking his eyes from the swirling, ever moving prisms and arcs of color that filled the body of the old church.

But that dance was only a curtain raiser for the animals. To a slower beating of the drums, in lumbered a herd of buffalo. The dancers had painted their torsos black. Their heads and shoulders were covered with buffalo pelts. To the tip of each horn was fastened a fluff of eagle feathers. In one hand each dancer carried a rattle gourd and in the other a bow and arrow.

They danced slowly and majestically to the heavy hoofbeating of the drums. The thick walls of the old church vanished. Such was the magic of the dance that we were transported in a whisk out to the limitless plains where the "hunchbacked cattle" were lords of all.

Suddenly the tempo of the drums became lighter and faster. In came the deer. These dancers were bent over short canes to make them look like quadrupeds. On their heads, deer horns were fastened in a headdress. Their steps in contrast to the buffaloes' majestic pantomime were dainty and graceful. How human beings bent over short sticks could so give the impression of the shy creatures of the forest is a mystery. They sniffed curiously at imaginary shrubs, they nibbled imaginary tender leaves, their heads bent to one side as if savoring the flavor. They listened, taut as wires, to suspected dangers and skipped at full speed to imaginary shelter with the stiff-legged gait of deer fleeing down a mountainside.

Toward the end of the dance, buffalo and deer approached nearer and nearer to the high altar. Some mounted the steps. In a manger lay *El Santo Niño* —the Holy Child. Animals of the forest and plains presented the Child with sprigs of the sacred blue spruce, the symbol of everlasting life. Then they lumbered or skipped out of the old Franciscan church.

Dazed by color, sound, and imagery, we found our way back through the village to the parked car and watched blanketed Indians return to their cubical homes along the old river of romance. The lopsided moon had disappeared. Only the early morning Christmas stars lighted the dim hills and dimmer mountains as we rolled back toward Santa

Fe. It was four o'clock on Christmas morning. We had attended midnight mass in an unspoiled Franciscan church. We had been out on the Great Plains with the buffalo. We had visited the dappled forests of our pristine wilderness where deer skitter through light and shadow.

We had seen Earth Mother sped along her way in the rhythm of the seasons toward sunnier days and seed-planting time. We had known some of the joy that was here when the earth was young.

A Wide House and Hearth

Mrs. Apodaca does not approve of one woman living alone in a little adobe house. "Señora," she inquires frequently, "are you not often solitaria?"

Then to show me how one wise woman filled her empty house with people, she told me the story of Señora Garcia de Barranca. "Señora Garcia de Barranca," explained Mrs. Apodaca, settling herself comfortably in the big rocker for a prolonged session, "find herself leeving alone een quite beeg adobe. She ees weedow weeth leetle money and all her cheeldren are married and een own homes. Thees would never happen een good old days.

"So Señora Garcia de Barranca take leetle half-orphan Indian boy to board and go to school een Santa Fe. Hees name ees Tall Blue Spruce and he have eight years. Then Señora Garcia de Barranca's next to youngest daughter, Serafina, find herself also a weedow weeth baby girl-child, Rosa María, to support. Serafina find good job een Phoenix, Arizona, and her mamá takes leetle Rosa María eento her home. After four years, Señora Garcia de Barranca steel have Indian boy, Tall Blue Spruce, and leetle grandchild, Rosa María, weeth her."

Mrs. Apodaca and I refreshed ourselves with fruit juice and lemon cookies as the saga promised to continue for some time. At last she revived enough to continue.

"When leetle *Indio*, Tall Blue Spruce, have twelve years and leetle Rosa María have four, the youngest daughter, Dolores, her husband, and tween babies, Ramón and Pomposo, come to leeve weeth Señora Garcia de Barranca. The husband of thees youngest daughter ees *muy aristocrático* and what you Anglos call 'high-strung.' He have to stop work from time to time and 'get away from eet all' and take leetle treep. But they have nothing to treep een but old *troque*. Son-een-law *aristocrático* want to buy cream-colored Fordcito. So Señora Garcia de Barranca take them all een her house so youngest daughter, Dolores, can work and make payments on new cream-colored Fordcito weeth jumper seats.

"Then one terrible day, Señora Garcia de Barranca get letter from mamá of leetle Rosa María. Eet say she have found new job een San Francisco, California. She have also found new husband and they both want leetle Rosa María to come and leeve weeth them. They weel put her een nice nursery school so her mamá can keep her job. Letter have check to pay for railroad ticket.

"Señora Garcia de Barranca collapse. She love leetle Rosa María like her own child. Maybe more! But *naturalmente* ees best for Rosa María to have papá as well as mamá. But how can Señora Garcia de Barranca travel to San Francisco and back alone to take Rosa María to her own mamá and new papá?

"But the husband *aristocrático* of the youngest daughter, Dolores, have idea. He is about to have one of hees high-strung times. They weel use the money sent for railroad ticket and all go to San Francisco een cream-colored Fordcito, all of them, even leetle Tall Blue Spruce. They find Rosa María's mamá and new papá leeving een furnished apartment een nize part of town. They make beds on floor and all crowd een some way. But leetle Rosa María does not know mamá and new papá. She weel not seet on any lap but her grandmamá's.

"After a day or two of thees, the new papá say to Señora Garcia de Barranca, 'I do not like thees city life any better than thees baby does. I am good New Mexican from the veelage of Galisteo. So my wife and I talk it over and we say ees not good to take leetle Rosa María away from her grandmamá and her cousins, Ramón and Pomposo, and the leetle *Indio*, Tall Blue Spruce. We, too, weel move back to Santa Fe and leeve weeth grandmamá.' "

Mrs. Apodaca fluttered her hands and rolled her eyes heavenward. "So Rosa María's mamá and new papá crowd eento new cream-colored Fordcito and all their belongings were roped on top of car because every eench of room eenside was taken up weeth beeg peoples, and tween boys, Ramón and Pomposo, and leetle *Indio*, Tall Blue Spruce, and leetle Rosa María who begeen to smile at her mamá and new papá—from her grandmamá's lap, of course.

"Rosa María's mamá and new papá find work een Santa Fe, but pay not so good as een San Francisco. But weeth the son-in-law *aristocrático* and hees wife, Dolores, working, there were four wage-earners in the family and no rent to pay. Rosa María's new papá turned out to be a good man in the garden and fruit orchard. You never see such corn, chile, and tender *calabazas*. They had to build a new adobe storeroom for all their canned and dried fruit and vegetables.

"But as *los muchachos* grew beeger and beeger, they could not all crowd eento that cream-colored Fordcito. So they turn eet een for a beeg, blue station wagon. You should see eet on Sunday veesitings weeth every *muchacho* sailing bright-colored balloons out of weendows! They look like circus on parade.

"And son-in-law *aristocrático* do not have those high-strung times now. He just seets and watches TV pictures from faraway lands. He ees calm and *contento*.

"We Spanish like the beeg, beeg family and many peoples around us. Een old days when son or daughter married, they deed not move away. They just built a couple of rooms from end wall of parents' house. If there were many sons and daughters, the added rooms stretched way across the lot, on both sides."

Piñata Party

Swathed like a mummy in her heaviest shawl, Mrs. Apodaca came blowing into the Little Adobe House one evening after Christmas. "Ah," she complained, sinking into the big rocker before the red-flamed corner fireplace. "Where you been all through Chreesmas time, Señora? I know! You keep Chreesmas weeth *los Indios.*"

"The week before Christmas I did travel hundreds of miles back and forth to Zuñi Pueblo," I confessed. "I saw the great masked Shalakos after they came down from their mountaintop. We were allowed to enter a new, red-rock, Indian home and we saw the ancient rites of blessing a new Zuñi home."

"Where were you all Chreesmas week?" demanded Mrs. Apodaca.

"I did see a Rainbow Dance at Tesuque on Christmas Day and a Deer Dance at Santo Domingo the day after New Year," I had to acknowledge.

"Maybe you like the way of *los Indios* better than our way of old Spain," suggested Mrs. Apodaca straight of back and firm of lip. "Maybe you join Indian tribe and go live een some old pueblo."

"I saw a lot of the old Spanish ways," I protested. "I never saw so many *farolitos* used in all my life. There were hundreds and thousands of them all over town, not only on the rooftops and along adobe walls, but outlining driveways and tracing lot boundaries. The whole town was a stencil of saffron light from the paper-bag lanterns etched against the dark-blue winter sky."

Mrs. Apodaca rocked happily for a few minutes and then exclaimed, "But you missed *la piñata* party of Mees Boggers! Mees Emily was there. Mees Boggers wore a red and gold fiesta dress and so much silver and turquoise jewelry that I couldn't tell her from the Chreesmas tree.

"That party, Señora, get off to strange start and end to crash-bang of broken pottery. Mees Boggers had invited ten *muchachos* she knew from one of the Indian pueblos and ten from Tenorio Flat and ten leetle Anglos.

"All day I work making turkey sandwiches. 'We'll give them something sensible at first,' says Mees Boggers, 'and then the ice cream, cookies and hot chocolate.' So I pass beeg tray of turkey sandwiches to Indian children first. Every one of those leetle *Indios* shake head and look sad into empty plate. Spanish and Anglo children fill plates, eat and say, 'Yummy!'

"I go out and tale Mees Boggers not one leetle *Indio* weel eat turkey sandwich. Each one say same theeng when she send me back to ask what kind of meat they like in sandwich. Each one say 'sheep.' I go back and tale Mees Boggers and she almost scream. 'Can I roast a sheep at this stage of the game?' She ees excite.

"Mees Emily swish long skirts into kitchen and say, 'The turkey is a ceremonial bird in some pueblos. Indians would not think of eating it. You've lived here long enough to know that, Melora Boggers.'

"Then up dash Young Mr. Abeyta and Carmencita. 'Get bread ready with wild plum jelly on one side. We ride bikes to Benito's store to buy jar of peanut butter.' In no time they are back and Indian *muchachos* are eating sandwiches and saying

'Yummy!' They also eat ice cream and cookies and drink hot chocolate. Everyone ees happy.

"So then Mees Boggers say they weel break *la piñata*." As I knew, the *piñata* is a clay jar decorated with beads and flowers. It is hung from a ceiling beam and is filled with little presents and goodies. Each child is blindfolded and given a long pole with which he tries to hit and break the *piñata*. "But, of course, Señora, Mees Boggers had to get the finest *piñata* ever seen in Santa Fe. She drive way down to Juarez on the Mexican border to get the beegest and the best and the nicest theengs to put een eet."

Mrs. Apodaca groaned and sat stiff and straight in the big rocker. "That *piñata* would not break, Señora. Eet was so beeg and strong! Some of the beegest *muchachos* hit it hard, but eet would not break and scatter gifts. Some of the leetle *muchachos* began to weep bitter tears. Mees Boggers ees more and more excite.

"Then Young Mr. Abeyta and Carmencita disappear. Een few minutes they are back weeth the beeg pole that I use to prop my clothesline. Young Meester Abeyta heets *la piñata* a mighty blow. Eet breaks and pottery flies een every direction and down scatter leetle toys and candies and nuts.

Los muchachos shriek with joy and hop around peeking up the treasures."

We both sat watching the red piñon flames painting the white walls with rose-tipped shadows.

At last Mrs. Apodaca exclaimed, "That Mees Boggers ees the most excite person I know. I go back every day since that party to help get house nice. Every day I find pieces of *piñata* and clay dust in new places. There ees no end. Mees Boggers find some een her cup of coffee thees morning!"

Christmas Card from Santa Fe

For miles and miles around this part of New Mexico, over the coppery hills, march green-uniformed piñon forests. They look like rollicking little soldiers holding the land against all foes. Between them straggle their tatterdemalion campfollowers, the ragged-barked cedar trees, brazenly sporting their loot of purple berries and huge wayfarers' bundles of pink-tinted New Mexico mistletoe. Higher up in the mountains, the regular army of yellow pine, silver fir, and spruce marches in dignity toward the snowy summits and stands sentry duty against the wintry sky.

In spite of the grandeur of the regular army of evergreens, it is the Lilliputian piñon and ragged cedar that move into the Little Adobe House at Christmas. They are as simple, unassuming, and indigenous as the little house itself. Going after their greenery has become a kind of sprightly pilgrimage.

One year, an early snow had disappeared from Santa Fe, but on the north side of hills, not five miles from town, we wallowed to boottops in white, crusty windrows. We saw rabbit tracks and the incisive imprint of deer hoofs and something that looked very much like bear paddings. The blue-feathered *piñonero* defied this invasion of his domain with widespread sky-tinted wings and raucous imprecations. Came the click of busy clippers, the rasp of a small saw removing the gray limb of a cedar to which the pink-pearled, parasitic mistletoe clings.

One does not just gather greenery on these pilgrimages, one gathers a sense of unlimited, unpeopled space filled with countless gradations of color spilling in all directions from an overflowing beaker. One gathers mesatops, flat and wind-burnished, rising like terraces toward some Never-Never Land. One collects mountain peaks, wrapped like Indian shamans in white ceremonial blankets while they perform some mysterious rite of colored sands dribbled from practiced fingertips.

Even during the war years, when there was no gasoline for such frivolities as gathering Christmas greens, the little house had its customary decorations. I walked. With folded blanket under my arm, I trudged up slippery Chamisa Road and out to the hills. There I filled the big blanket with greenery, tied containing four corners together, slung the load over my shoulder, and trudged home looking like an Indian woman carrying a huge load of pottery.

In years of unlimited piñon gleanings, I insert them twig by twig all along the cinnamon-brown, pine-tree vigas. Part of the green fronds reach to the ceiling and others drape themselves downward. The pink-berried mistletoe balls attached to ragged, twisted branches are suspended by stout cords to white-walled room corners. They outline doorways and deep-set casement windows. They curve along the corner fireplace. In a southern window the Christmas cactus blooms after a year of pampering. It shows layers of dark-green fronds among whose leaves red, fuchsia-like flowers bloom only during the Christmas season.

When paper-bag lanterns glow like orange parchment along outside window ledges, beside the narrow walk to the front door, and atop a low adobe wall, when the corner fireplace hums its song of deep content, when white walls flush with reflected flame, then the pine-draped ceiling turns the room into a forest bower, dark, mysterious, and fragrant. One would not be at all surprised to see a spotted fawn peer from a dark corner.

Tall turquoise candles are lighted. In the dim forest-filled room there is enough polished copper scattered about to double or triple their flames. On one of the tiered shelves of the fireplace stands an "Indian Christmas tree." Why it should be called that, I do not know. I doubt if any real Indian would recognize it. It is a small yucca plant embedded in a deep, heavy crock. On every one of the thorns, at the end of each slender frond, is impaled a red (probably New England) cranberry. Indian or not, it delights the eye.

That most elegant feline, El Hijo de Koshare, in his adobe-colored winter ruff, wanders about the transformed room sniffing the forest scents with quivering whiskers. He scouts behind chairs and prowls along the top of bookcases. He leaps to the windowsill and stares out at *los farolitos* flickering in the wintry gusts. He examines the "Indian Christmas tree" much as an archaeologist examines "find." When no one is looking he manages to remove one of the cranberries, drops it to the floor, and pursues it into dark corners.

When a tap comes on the door, he dashes under the little red sofa to show his disinclination for intrusions. When to the fragrance of piñon branches along the ceiling and piñon flames in the fireplace is added the beguiling scent of cinnamon-spiced hot chocolate and Christmas cookies, he forgets his isolationist instincts and saunters out to accept a sample of Christmas cake and to steal three more cranberries from the "Indian Christmas tree."

Muchachos with eyes like stars line up outside the uncurtained window, knowing full well that cookies will appear at the door. Cousin Canuto ambles by and signals a greeting with the flash of a homemade lantern of candle in an old tin can. Mrs. Apodaca raps at the window and waves. Young Mr. Abeyta clumps by on the old horse of his papá.

The fire burns to red coals. Candles are snuffed

and El Hijo de Koshare retires to his cushioned chair. Just to be on the safe side, I remove the "Indian Christmas tree" to a very high shelf. He watches me with "deesdain." This is the way it has been in the Little Adobe House, with slight variations, for many Chistmases. But always it seems new and sparkling.

The Approach Diplomatico

Señora, confided Mrs. Apodaca, "our Cousin Canuto have the fine new way of theenking and doing. But eet weel not work! Hees leetle store, the boys' newspaper beesness, even María Lupita's wash machine wheech she rent to other señoras to make leetle money—all are een way to collapse."

"What has Cousin Canuto thought up now?" I questioned.

"The Approach *Diplomático*," groaned Mrs.

Apodaca. "Many peoples do not pay cash for theengs they buy een leetle store. When boys' newspaper customers weel not pay, the boys have to be *diplomático* and they get no money. Neighbors who use wash machine do not pay one cent even for what juice electrica costs. ¡*Ay de mí*!

"My Cousin Canuto ees educate man. He read and write een Spanish and een English. He buy leetle book wheech tale how to use the approach *diplomático*. So poor María Lupita and four nize boys een newspaper beesness have to do the approach *diplomático*. Eet ruin them all!"

"What does that little book tell them to say?"

"I theenk eet tale them to say what they do not mean, and een *muchas, muchas palabras*—many, many words."

It was a day of blue and gold and soft feathery snow as I walked up the path that led to Cousin Canuto's casita. Chile con carne was simmering gently on the old wood-burning stove. María Lupita was waiting on a neighbor who was selecting many groceries from the depleted shelves of the little store at the end of the room. Cousin Canuto was writing a letter, evidently *diplomático*, as the crawling pace of his pen indicated.

"Some of those picture-taking people from

back East, want me to guide them again this summer," he explained, signing the long letter. "Listen, Señora, see if you think I have answered with the approach *diplomático*."

Cousin Canuto, with apparent pride in his masterpiece, read the three-page-long epistle which skirted dates, shied around prices, and avoided places with studied indefiniteness.

"It's a friendly letter," I said, as he ended. "but why so vague? You know perfectly well when you can guide them and what it will cost. One short paragraph would do it."

Cousin Canuto sighed at my stupidity. "In the approach *diplomático* you make the other person think he is doing all the thinking. It is the kind way."

In the quiet that followed, I heard María Lupita say to the customer in the little store, "Señora Ulibarri, you now owe us feefty dollars and your husband have good job. Eef you do not pay us a leetle, I cannot let you take those theengs home."

Cousin Canuto fairly flew across the room to the wooden counter. "Excuse María Lupita, Señora Ulibarri," he begged. "She have little head for things financial. Please take the groceries with you. I will put your credit slip on the nail with your others. And come back when you need more."

María Lupita threw herself into the big chair and tears ran down her cheeks. "Señora Ulibarri tale me last week that they cannot pay us because they buy four new tires for their *carro*. But the wholesale peoples tale us last week that eef we get any more theengs for our store, eet weel be cash or nussings. Ees nussings!"

At that minute, in burst the oldest boy in the newspaper business. "Papá," he gasped, "I said just what you told me to say to Mrs. Ledderbetter. But she didn't pay me a cent for all the papers I've pushed on my bike up that hill where she lives. So I went down to her husband's store and told him what was what."

Cousin Canuto shuddered, but his son continued. "He paid up everything, and a month in advance. I deliver the paper to his store from now on. Gosh, Papá, that approach *diplomático* is the berries!"

When I walked into my driveway at nightfall, Mrs. Apodaca, swathed to her nosetip, was stalking up and down like a lioness. "Wasn't eet just the way as I say, Señora? The leetle store ruin? The boys' newspaper beesness ruin. María Lupita collapse?"

Two weeks later, Cousin Canuto appeared in Casita Apodaca. We were talking of the early spring and the whir of migrating bird wings over our houses all day. But Cousin Canuto looked neither spring-like nor happy. "Ah, Señora, I get letter from picture-taking gentlemen back East. They say they get nice letter from some guide in Colorado who tell them just when and how much their summer trip will cost. They will go to Colorado."

After this sad news, he pulled a big card from under his arm. "The wholesale grocery people," he sighed. "They say it has to go up over my grocery shelves behind the counter. They will not sell me any more groceries if I do not put up this terrible sign. And do just as they say!" No Credit, it proclaimed in large letters.

Then he called to Carmencita, "*Por favor,* to type me a little card for María Lupita's business of renting wash machine. Say at top in big letters, Rules for Using Wash Machine, and under it in big letters, Fifty Cents an Hour."

At this, Mrs. Apodaca interrupted. "And, Carmencita, poot under that een beeg letters, Paid Een Advance!"

Cousin Canuto smiled. "I learn lesson hard way. I think to be *diplomático* is to be kind. But maybe it is more kind to tell people just where they stand when questions come up. And it does not take so many words!"

"*Sí*," nodded Mrs. Apodaca, "ees more kind to tale them point of the blank."

Ships of the Desert

One cold, snow-filled evening, Cousin Canuto, Mrs. Apodaca, and I were sitting around my corner fireplace. Mrs. Apodaca was showing me the only Christmas card she had saved. It pictured three caparisoned camels bearing the Three Wise Men over desert wastes under the guidance of a great star.

Cousin Canuto appeared somewhat bored with this return to Christmas. Every once in a while he broke into the conversation with the competitive subject of the long, Indian-contested journeys the early settlers in this region made once or twice a year to faraway Chihuahua in Old Mexico.

"That long, danger-fraught journey was dramatic," I agreed, "but I can tell you a story of Anglos here—not so long ago, in the 1850's—that was not particularly dangerous, but which was one of the most fantastic happenings in this country. Your Christmas card with the camels made me think of it."

"Tale us, Señora," begged Mrs. Apodaca, tossing her black shawl from her shoulders. "Tale us the story *fantástica*."

"Did you ever see a big animal with a hump on his back called a camel?" I questioned.

"Once when I was a boy, I saw one in a circus parade in Albuquerque," nodded Cousin Canuto.

"Only on Chreesmas cards," sighed Mrs. Apodaca.

The story I told them is one of the strangest in all American history. It has its pathos and its humor. Very few Americans know anything about it.

We Anglo-Americans in the 1850's were settling in the West—California, Arizona, and New Mexico. There were no railroads in this part of the

West then. Nothing but high mountains and, in between, vast expanses of desert, often with waterholes many miles apart. Even when travelers on horseback or muleback found a waterhole, it would be dried to nothing but sandy waste and slime. Horses and mules perished.

At last, a Navy lieutenant, Edward F. Beale, had a brilliant thought. If part of the West was more or less desert, why not get some camels to freight things over the desert sands? He had experienced that desert himself when he was taking dispatches to Washington from the West. The mule he was riding had nearly perished from thirst on that desert.

It took some time for Congress to decide that it would spend all of $30,000 for camels to be brought here from the Middle East. In a first shipment, thirty-four camels reached the Southwest in 1856, only about a hundred years ago. Later, forty-one more arrived and ten camel drivers, one of whom was named Hadji Ali, which name was soon changed to Hi Jolly!

At first, everything seemed to go well. The camels plodded over the desert with much heavier loads than horses or mules could carry. Often they made twenty-five to thirty miles a day. They could climb mountains, swim streams, and would eat kinds of desert vegetation which horses and mules would not touch even when starving.

"Just like an Anglo to think up something like that," exclaimed Cousin Canuto.

"It didn't turn out so well," I said. "The camels seemed to feel at home on the American desert, but the camel drivers didn't do so well. One by one they returned to their own desert lands."

"What deed U Esse do then?" begged Mrs. Apodaca.

"They brought in United States Army mule skinners."

Cousin Canuto roared with laughter at that.

The mule skinners did not understand that the skills in handling horses and mules would not work out with camels from the East. Even people driving horses and mules across the desert had a hard time, as their mules and horses stampeded in absolute terror when they saw the great humpbacked exotic animals. And of course the camels did not understand words of command given them in mule skinner English.

Then came the Civil War and the country could not be concerned with camels. A few of them were sold, but most of them were turned loose on the desert. There they and their offspring ran free for many years. Cattle stampeded at the very scent of them. People new to the desert thought they had lost their minds when they saw camels cavorting across the desert sands of America.

"Ay," shuddered Cousin Canuto, "how would you like to stop at a desert waterhole and look up to see three or four great beasts rolling their eyes and switching their tails when they discovered you?"

The last one reported was seen in 1913, not so long ago. Probably hunters, hungry Indians, or coyotes accounted for the rest. But the strange feature of the story is that nature had prepared a monument for them. It is a rocky formation east of Phoenix, Arizona, known as Camelback Mountain. Seen at one angle, this ruddy mountain looks very much like a huge camel squatting on its knees.

After learning all this about camels on our desert, I realized years later that Santa Fe also has its rock camel only a few miles along the highway north of town. In the tourist season, it is a favorite place for people to have their pictures taken against the almost pink camel—even if they know nothing about the original camels.

"Oh," applauded Mrs. Apodaca, "You Anglos do have a leetle *historia* that sounds a leetle like our *tradiciones*."

A Caravan of Christmas

With my twenty-fifth Christmas in New Mexico, I am realizing more and more how deeply permeated all of them have been with customs and delights quite foreign to my background and previous experience. It all started on the first Christmas here when a friend and I climbed the great rock of Acoma to have dinner with an Indian family in the tawny pueblo etched against the turquoise sky. It has continued gradually and naturally through a quarter of a century until now the strands of Indian, Spanish, and Anglo are difficult to disentangle.

Even the corner fireplace, garlanded with piñon greens and lighted by tall blue candles, which is the center of all homekeeping joys, was originally designed by an Anglo woman and built by an Indian.

The little shops around our wintry plaza carry gifts that could only originate in the area—wood carvings by a descendant of famous craftsmen, woven bags, purses and blankets hand-loomed in the Spanish villages, cottonwood and rawhide drums from Cochiti, turquoise and silver jewelry hammered out by Navajo and Zuñi silversmiths, famous black pottery from San Ildefonso, and brown wares from Zia.

The buying of one another's wares is general, I noticed last Christmas when I watched an Indian couple shopping in a chain store for a doll evidently intended for their little girl. At least, the blanket-wrapped mother was shopping while the father stood somewhat ill at ease at a distance as nearly all fathers do. On the long counter were many dolls—dolls dressed as Indians, black mammy dolls, white dolls, both blonde and brunette.

The Indian woman picked them up one by one

and examined them carefully. She discarded the black mammy dolls, she discarded the brunette white dolls. At last, smiling happily, she held up for her husband's approval a blonde doll with yellow curls, blue eyes, and pink cheeks. The Indian man gazed at this very blonde doll and suddenly burst into laughter punctuated by staccato exclamations in Tewa. But the Indian woman produced a flat old purse from which she extracted two much-folded dollar bills. Thus did a very blonde doll baby go home to some bronze-tinted little girl in an old adobe pueblo along the Rio Grande.

One year when we were driving toward Taos on a lowering, snow-threatening afternoon before Christmas, we passed a lonely ranch and saw a small Spanish American boy laying up logs for *las luminarias* along the rutted thread of road that led to a sagging adobe house. It seemed a poor home for Christmas. But as we looked back from the top of the hill, we saw that the little piñon fires had been lighted. They cast a glory of rosy flame over the poor little place that turned it into something to remember.

Indians have always danced at the turn of the solstice. They dance from Christmas Eve through New Year's Day, but when, where, or what is often hard to determine in advance. "Let's go out and see what dances they are giving," is the usual procedure. The result is that we roll miles and miles up and down the Rio Grande in a delightful state of adventure and are overjoyed if we find a children's dance at Santo Domingo or stumble on a Deer Dance at Tesuque in the crimson afterglow of a winter sunset.

For many years, a great electric star shone on top of Atalaya Hill not far from the Little Adobe House. Nearly every night during the Christmas season, I walked out beside the leafless lilac hedge, under the real stars in the wintry sky, to feast my eyes on that huge man-made star atop the little hill.

Just in itself it was heart-filling. But knowing the story of that hill makes it many times more lovely and poignant. This little Spanish and Anglo settlement in the shadow of great mountains knew a terrible isolation through the years. But when Yankee traders began roaring down the Santa Fe Trail in covered wagons, this outpost of Old Spain and Mexico began to have contact with a whole new world.

Whenever the time approached that a caravan of covered wagons might be expected, watchers were sent to the top of Atalaya Hill to give the adobe settlement warning that visitors might be expected. When the first wagon came in view, the watchers ran at full speed into the adobe settlement shouting, "*La caravana, la caravana!*"

Everyone in the settlement raced to the plaza to see the travel-battered wagons pull in with their cargoes of calico, sugar, shoes, slippers for dancing feet, and pieces of glass to go into little house windows that had only known a thin piece of mica. It was a time for dances, for meeting old friends and seeing new faces. It was people meeting people. This all added luster to that bright man-made star which I could see from my small wedge of New Mexico soil. What a *caravana* of races, cultures, and people is Christmas in Santa Fe!